Praxis II Health and Physical Education Content Knowledge (5857) Exam

"You never fail until you stop trying" - Albert Einstein

For inquiries;
info@xmprep.com

Praxis II Health and Physical Education Content Knowledge (5857) Exam #1

Test Taking Tips

☐ Take a deep breath and relax

☐ Read directions carefully

☐ Read the questions thoroughly

☐ Make sure you understand what is being asked

☐ Go over all of the choices before you answer

☐ Paraphrase the question

☐ Eliminate the options you know are wrong

☐ Check your work

☐ Think positively and do your best

Table of Contents

TEST DIRECTION

Read the questions carefully and then choose the ONE best answer to each question.

Be sure to allocate your time carefully so you are able to complete the entire test within the testing session. You may go back and review your answers at any time.

You may use any available space in your test booklet for scratch work.

Questions in this booklet are not actual test questions but they are the samples for commonly asked questions.

This test aims to cover all topics which may appear on the actual test. However some topics may not be covered.

Studying this booklet will be preparing you for the actual test. It will not guarantee improving your test score but it will help you pass your exam on the first attempt.

Some useful tips for answering multiple choice questions;

- Start with the questions that you can easily answer.

- Underline the keywords in the question.

- Be sure to read all the choices given.

- Watch for keywords such as NOT, always, only, all, never, completely.

- Do not forget to answer every question.

1

Trunk extension is a type of exercise that aims to 'undo' the excessive slumping of your trunk or back. The back muscles are stretched enough to retain its form, from the neck to the spine.

Which of the following component of physical fitness does this activity assess?

A) Balance

B) Flexibility

C) Coordination

D) Body endurance

2

A **bowling** ball has to be rolled in the alley and reach the end of it to hit the pins arranged in a set manner. The score is based on the number of pins hit in an attempt.

Which of the following is the ruling for an accidental hit for the last pin by a mechanical pinsetter?

A) Foul

B) Replay

C) Reset frame

D) No point awarded

3

Weightlifting refers to the activity that involves heavyweights such as barbel.

Which of the following exercise principle is applied when trainees add more repetitions to a weightlifting set?

A) Overload

B) Flexibility

C) Progression

D) Adaptability

2

CONTINUE ▶

4

Extrinsic   Intrinsic

Motivation is derived from the word motive in the English language which is defined as a need that requires satisfaction. In the educational setting, motivation is either an internal force or external force that is used within the educational system to encourage student learning and understanding.

Which of the following about the motivation is not correct?

A) Motivation is the reason for people's actions, willingness and goals.

B) Motivation is the intrinsic and extrinsic factors that stimulate people to take actions that lead to achieving a goal.

C) Intrinsic motivation comes from the satisfaction derived from working on and completing a task.

D) Extrinsic motivation stems directly from an action rather than a reward associated with working on a task.

5

Eye contact is a form of nonverbal communication and is thought to have a large influence on social behavior.

Why is it necessary for a speaker to make eye contact with the members of the audience?

A) It creates a bond of distrust.

B) It tells the audience that the speaker is dishonest.

C) It results in the audience to be less likely engaged in the discussion.

D) It establishes the speakers confidence about the material he/she is discussing to the audience.

6

Stress is a critical factor in assessing the performance of athletes and students. Most students that are negatively affected by stress perform below average during physical education.

Which of the following is not a common negative stressor?

A) Loss of income
B) Death of a family member
C) Successive injuries in the game
D) Conflict in interpersonal relationships

7

Which of the following is not one of the benefits of physical activity?

A) Social benefit; physical activity can help develop friendships.
B) Physical benefit; physical activity can help to relieve tension and contributes to weight loss.
C) Mental benefit; physical activity improves blood glucose control in type 2 diabetes.
D) Health benefit; regular physical activity can prevent high blood pressure, help arthritis.

8

Doing an exercise can be more efficient and handy by using the proper type of equipment according to your developmental goals. For example weight lifts can be used to develop your muscles.

Which of the following exercise equipment best applies the physiological principles?

A) Rolling machine
B) Stationary bicycle
C) Electrical muscle stimulator
D) Motor-driven rowing machine

9

Activities in which players send an object toward an object while avoiding any obstacles are called target game.

A target game is best illustrated by which of the following games?

A) Racing
B) Fencing
C) Bocce
D) Indoor court game

10

Formative Assessment has been described as "ongoing" and takes place during teaching-learning situations in physical education(PE).

Which of the following about Formative assessment in PE is correct?

A) It provides vital information for summative assessment.

B) It is closely related to "Assessment for Learning" and it has been commended for its emphasis on describing progress, identifying pupils' needs, planning for next steps.

C) It involves providing pupils with constructive feedback, diagnosing future learning needs, describing students' progress, and determining their strengths and weaknesses.

D) All of the above

11

Non-locomotor skills focus on using the body to stay physically fit. The muscles are stretched or used in a well-mannered way so that they can be utilized more efficiently in the future.

Which of the following non-locomotor skills is developed by activities such as picking fruits from trees as well as "plucking the stars from the sky"?

A) Bending
B) Turning
C) Twisting
D) Stretching

12

Exercising helps the body regulate the energy intake from the food that is consumed. The energy is then converted into different forms, which can be used by the body's growth.

Which of the following is not a physiological benefit of exercise?

A) Improved appearance
B) Improved quality of life
C) Improved sleeping patterns
D) Improved energy regulation

13

Maintaining a proper and suitable weight is important to perform physical activities requiring speed or endurance. Instructors want students to maintain a suitable weight where they can perform better in physical education.

Which of the following can be recommended first for an obese student whose fitness assessments is poor for every component of fitness?

A) A walking program
B) A running program
C) A stretching program
D) An intensity-based program

14

Target games are activities in which players send an object toward a target while avoiding any obstacles.

Which of the following sports is the best example of a target game?

A) Bocce
B) Badminton
C) Basketball
D) Lacrosse

15

An instructor must prescribe a sufficient number of exercises for a player to develop his motor skills rapidly. The basics of acquiring a locomotor skill depend on the player's determination as well.

Which of the following locomotor skills is developed by taking off and landing with both feet together?

A) Hopping
B) Jumping
C) Leaping
D) Skipping

CONTINUE ▶

16

Health-related physical fitness is made up of five components. The components of health-related physical fitness are muscular strength, muscular endurance, flexibility, cardiorespiratory endurance, and body composition.

Which of the following about health-related physical fitness and activities is not correct?

A) Females are less likely to show high skill levels in physical activities.

B) When beginning a new fitness routine some muscle aches and pains are not normal.

C) A lack of confidence is often given as a reason for non-participation in physical activities.

D) Watching an Olympic athlete and joining an athletics' club is the best example of a role model promoting participation in physical activities.

17

A measurement showing the **"average differences"** from what most people score on a test refers to which of the following ?

A) Mean

B) Mode

C) Median

D) Standard deviation

18

Product assessment is an outcome-based assessment in physical education. The student performs, and the instructor objectively assesses according to the standards.

Which of the following is true for product assessment?

A) It measures an individual's skill

B) It evaluates student performance

C) It gives insight in correcting student's errors

D) All of the above

19

The body's balance is important in playing a sport. A balanced movement and physical body help the player perform a skill in a better condition.

Which of the following does not enhance equilibrium?

A) Lowering the base of support

B) Increasing the base of support

C) Increasing the base of support and lowering the center of support

D) Shifting the center of gravity away from the direction of movement

20

Class participation must be maintained at a prescribed level to ensure that the students are engaged in the lesson. If the participation is low, the instructor must be able to cope with that case.

Which of the following concepts can be used to enhance class participation?

A) Multi-activity designs

B) Activity modification

C) Heterogeneous grouping

D) Homogeneous grouping

21

Team building activities are based on social interaction. This promoted the cohesiveness of the team members but being aware of their different personalities.

Which of the following sports does not enhance team socialization?

A) Golf

B) Football

C) Volleyball

D) Basketball

22

A tournament can be a city-wide event or regional event. The scope of the event is dependent on the host.

Which of the following is not a type of tournament?

A) Pyramid
B) Spiralistic
C) Spider web
D) Round robin

23

What is the most probably effect when overtraining in a college cross-country runner?

A) Decreased creatine kinase
B) Increased muscle glycogen
C) Increased lactate concentrations
D) Decreased percentage of body fat

24

There are three reference systems that have been used for assessment in physical education (PE). These are;

- Norm Referenced Assessment
- Criterion Referenced Assessment
- Ipsative Referenced Assessment

Which of the following about Criterion Referenced assessment in PE is correct?

A) It is regarded as "group centred", as comparisons within the group are made to establish how successful the pupil is in relation to others of the same age
B) It can be detrimental to students' self-esteem, as when pupils progress to "above average", it is at the expense of others who become "below average".
C) It has been criticised as in a high calibre class pupils may receive on average a lower mark, compared to a mediocre class who receives on average a higher mark
D) All of the above

25

Physical education has been developed by researching methods of improving the physical condition of youth in the US. During the war, it cannot be avoided that some of the youth are sent to the battlefield.

Which of the following physical education philosophy is based on experience?

A) Idealism
B) Naturalism
C) Pragmatism
D) Existentialism

26

A physical education class requires to develop the cognitive domain of the students. It is an essential part of the class as it aims to develop the brain and intellectual skills.

Which of the following is not an evaluation method for the cognitive domain?

A) Standardized Tests
B) Norm-Referenced Tests
C) Criterion Referenced Tests
D) Willis Sports Interaction Tests

27

Which of the following defines the state in which an object stays at rest or at motion unless a net force acts upon it?

A) Inertia
B) Balance
C) Action/Reaction
D) Symmetric Motion

28

The **cardio-respiratory system** involves the acquisition of oxygen to the working muscles and the removal of carbon dioxide from the body.

Which of the following will be least likely identified from cardio-respiratory assessment results?

A) Smoking history
B) Running endurance
C) Natural over-fatness
D) Functional aerobic capacity

29

A **sports meet** is an exclusive event for a range of participants in a class, school, or a small area. It is different from a tournament in the scale of its conduct.

Which of the following is not a type of sports meet?

A) Ladder
B) Extramural
C) Intramural
D) Interscholastic

30

Due to the diverse effects of physical education in the educational curriculum, different perspectives developed throughout its development. Their concepts are different but they aim to arrive at the same end.

Which of the following describes Idealism?

A) More on practice
B) Experience-based
C) The laws of nature
D) The mind is developed through acquisition of knowledge

31

Equilibrium is a condition in which all acting influences are canceled by others, resulting in a stable, balanced, or unchanging system.

Which of the following conditions maintain equilibrium?

A) The base of support is reduced.
B) The center of gravity is lowered.
C) The center of gravity is over the base of support.
D) Force is inversely proportional to support.

32

Which of the following exercises would promote core strength and endurance which is essential in back support and core stability?

A) Plank
B) Bicycle crunch
C) Abdominal curl-up
D) One arm toe touch crunch

33

Which of the following about sports is not correct?

A) Most sociologists describe sports as an institutionalized activity.
B) An activity becomes a sport if the organization becomes standardized over time.
C) Sports activities have official rule enforcement, equipment regulations, and formalized skills.
D) Learning about rules, traditions, history, and etiquette of sports belong to the psychomotor domain of learning.

34

An intensive workout or exercise can cause fatigue in the body. A cooling down exercise is recommended to be performed to help the body to lower down its activity to normal levels.

Which of the following is not a benefit of cooling down?

A) Preventing dizziness
B) Removing lactic acid
C) Removing myoglobin
D) Redistributing circulation

35

Aerobics is the energetic physical exercises that make the heart, lungs, and muscles stronger, It increases the amount of oxygen in the blood.

Which of the following about aerobic exercise, which is also known as cardio, is not correct?

A) Aerobics is best for improving cardiovascular health.
B) Anaerobic exercise is long-lasting, low-intensity activity.
C) Aerobic exercise promotes circulation throughout the blood.
D) Aerobics is an appropriate method of training to improve your flexibility.

36

Critical thinking is a clear, rational, open-minded and disciplined thinking informed by evidence.

Critical reasoning is the process of using critical thinking, knowledge & experience to find solutions to the problems.

Which of the following is recommended during the critical thinking process?

A) Willingness to ask questions
B) A good foundation of knowledge
C) Ability to recognize new answers
D) All of the above

37

Basketball Zone Defense

A basketball team has obtained an outstanding center that is highly skilled in rebounding. The coach intends to keep the player near the basket.

Which of the following strategies should the coach implement to keep the player near the basket?

A) Pick-and-roll
B) Zone defense
C) Free-lancing
D) Give-and-go

38

Which of the following is reduced by following the correct racing posture of a swimmer, a cyclist or a downhill skier?

A) Speed
B) Turbulence
C) Risk of injury
D) Gravitational force

39

Safety during physical education classes must be strictly observed by wearing the prescribed uniform, gear, and other necessary protective equipment. The student is also liable for his personal safety, aside from the guidance of the instructor.

Which of the following actions does not promote safety?

A) Presenting organized activities
B) Inspecting equipment and facilities
C) Instructing skills and activities properly
D) Allowing students to wear the current style of shoes

Progressive exercise is a safer way to develop a student's body. New students must aim to develop their bodies before they can consider intensive training gradually.

Which of the following principles of progression applies to improving muscle endurance?

A) Lifting weights every day

B) Lifting weights with low resistance and low reps

C) Lifting weights at 20% to 30% of assessed muscle strength

D) Lifting weights starting at 60% of assessed muscle strength

Isometric exercise is considered as a strength training in which the length of the muscle and joint angle do not change during contraction.

Which of the following is not correct about isometric exercise?

A) It can increase muscle strength at specific joint angles.

B) It contributes to building muscle and burning fat.

C) It always produces spikes in systolic blood pressure.

D) It can cause a life-threatening cardiovascular accident because it is done in one position without movement.

42

Locomotor skills are movement skills used by an individual to build coordination of the body. Walking and running are common locomotor skills that you can use daily.

Which of the following is the proper order of sequential development for the acquisition of locomotor skills?

A) Creep, crawl, walk, slide, run, hop, leap, skip, gallop, jump, step-hop

B) Creep, crawl, walk, jump, run, slide, gallop, hop, leap, skip, step-hop

C) Crawl, walk, creep, slide, walk, run, hop, leap, gallop, skip, step-hop

D) Crawl, creep, walk, run, jump, hop, gallop, slide, leap, skip, step-hop

43

Criterion Referenced Assessment compares pupils performance to a predetermined criteria or standard.

Which of the following about Criterion Referenced assessment in physical education is correct?

A) Criterion Referencing is an "activity centered" assessment.

B) It promotes collaborative learning as pupils are working together towards a common goal.

C) It provides educators with a more accurate measuring stick to assess pupils learning, and provides details of the additional work students must complete to reach the next level of achievement.

D) All of the above

44

Muscle development is an important aspect of physical training. The strength, endurance, and volume of your muscles can dictate the extent of training you can receive as well as the exercises you can perform for a period.

Which of the following is assessed to identify an individual's potential of developing musculoskeletal problems and performing activities of daily living?

A) Muscle Volume

B) Muscle flexibility

C) Muscle ednurance

D) Motor reaction speed

45

When a curriculum is being held, managing the class must be inclined with the principles of the course. An excellently planned curriculum must be able to manage the class while being able to achieve the developmental milestones.

Which of the following is not a class management technique in a physical education class?

A) Explaining conditioning

B) Promoting individual self-discipline

C) Explaining routines for changing and showering

D) Explaining procedures for roll call, excuses, and tardiness

46

What kind of activity primarily describes organized sports according to most sports sociologists?

A) Player friendly
B) Institutionalized
C) Family sports
D) Mind games

47

Which type of assessment objectively measures skill performance of a student?

A) Iowa Brace Test
B) Process assessment
C) Product assessment
D) Criterion-referenced tests

48

Fox and Hound is a game that requires the players to run rapidly. The schematic of the game lets the players move as fox while the hounds chase after the fox by following their signals.

Which of the following locomotor skill is developed by this catch-and-chase game?

A) Hopping
B) Skipping
C) Galloping
D) Stepping-hopping

49

Weight-bearing is the physical state of supporting an applied load while strength training is a type of physical exercise specializing in the use of resistance to induce muscular contraction which builds the strength, anaerobic endurance, and size of skeletal muscles.

Which of the following is the benefit of weight-bearing and strength training exercises to older adults?

A) Increase toned muscles
B) Increase respiration rate
C) Reduce the risk of fractures
D) Reduce the risk of coronary diseases

50

Skill and strategy performance comes hand in hand when playing for a sport. The level of the skill can determine the success of the strategy employed.

Which of the following techniques must be first learned to enhance skill and strategy performance for striking or throwing objects, for catching or collecting objects, and for carrying and propelling objects?

A) Offensive stance

B) Defensive stance

C) Controlling objects

D) Redirecting objects

51

In bowling, the main goal is to strike all the pins in as little balls as possible. If the pins do not fall in one attempt, you have to continue rolling balls until a given number of balls.

Which of the following is a bowling pin that remains standing after an apparently perfect hit?

A) Tap

B) Blow

C) Turkey

D) None of the above

52

For table tennis, a player may start practicing by hitting the ball towards the wall back and forth. A track and field player, on the other hand, can practice by jumping over objects of different heights.

Which of the following quality of movement is demonstrated by the training methods given above?

A) Time

B) Force

C) Inertia

D) Balance

53

Running in a series of workout that requires the body to adapt quickly. A running, lifting, and pull-up track can be placed in different orders for this type of training.

Which of the following quality of movement is demonstrated by finishing these set of workout in the fastest time possible?

A) Time

B) Force

C) Inertia

D) Balance

54

In the given choices, which activity is the most aerobically demanding in terms of kcal/hour burned?

A) Volleyball
B) Walking
C) Cross-country skiing
D) Bowling

55

A **vertical jump** is a kind of jump that is used to assess a student's highest vertical reach.

Which of the following component of fitness does a vertical jump activity assess?

A) Power
B) Balance
C) Strength
D) Endurance

56

Rules should be established to manage a physical education class. Discipline is an important matter in physical training.

Which of the following is not a class-management technique?

A) Explaining conditioning
B) Promoting individual self-discipline
C) Explaining routines for changing and showering
D) Explaining procedures for roll call, excuses, and tardiness

57

Aerobic and anaerobic exercises play their features depending on the type of training or goal set for the student. An instructor lays down instructions for an exercise such as warming up or cooling down.

Which of the following is a benefit of cooling down?

A) Increase in power
B) Heightened senses
C) Increased muscle tension
D) Redistributing circulation

A physical education curriculum must start at the basics like an introductory session to introduce the course. The teacher can plan ahead or follow the instruction manual if provided.

Which of the following must a PE teacher consider when planning his curriculum?

A) Student's hobbies

B) Student's schedule

C) Easiest exercises available

D) Equipment and available facilities

Children develop the ability to propel an object through the air with a rapid movement of the arm and wrist by projecting balls at progressively smaller targets.

Which of the following manipulative skills will children develop in the activity given above?

A) Bouncing

B) Throwing

C) Snapping

D) Trapping

CONTINUE ▶

Ipsative Referencing Assessment compares a pupil's current performance with his previous performance in the same activity.

Which of the following about Ipsative assessment in physical education is correct?

A) It is regarded as 'child centered', as pupils focus on beating their previous achievement, which is useful for recording learning and progress.

B) It promotes a mastery climate, again eliminating comparison with others, which enhances pupils' self-esteem, motivation, and accountability.

C) It provides a foundation for self and teacher assessments in Records of Achievement

D) All of the above

Body composition is used to describe the percentages of fat, bone, water, and muscle in human bodies.

To measure body composition, which of the following instruments would give the most accurate results?

A) Skin calipers

B) Tape measure

C) Balanced scale

D) T-ray detectors

Health, as defined by the World Health Organization (WHO), is "**a state of complete physical, mental and social well-being, and not merely the absence of disease or infirmity.** Achieving a balance of physical, spiritual, emotional, social, intellectual, and physical health is good health.

Which of the following terms about health-related physical fitness is not defined correctly?

A) Agility is the ability to move quickly and easily, get a quick start and leave the opposition behind.

B) Strength is a physical fitness component that can also help in following a healthy lifestyle.

C) Flexibility is the ability to increase the range of movements possible at a joint and hold a better technical shape.

D) Coordination is the ability to stay in control of body movement, and balance is the ability to move two or more body parts under control, smoothly and efficiently.

An **exercise** is a physical activity performed to maintain bodily wellness and health. It can enhance and develop the body towards a certain level.

Which of the following exercise training principle refers to working at a level above normal?

A) Intensity
B) Overload
C) Specificity
D) Performance

21

CONTINUE ▶

64

Rowing is a type of sport associated with boat racing. An individual or team have to row in a body of water while inside a boat to reach a certain distance or goal.

Which of the following is developed by rowing?

A) Balance
B) Reaction speed
C) Muscle flexibility
D) Muscle endurance

65

Cooling-down is the opposite of warming up and is intended to assist the body in returning to its normal resting state. Cool-down activities should be continued but at a lower intensity.

Which of the following about cooling-down activities is not correct?

A) They reduce the cholesterol level in the blood.
B) They prevent blood from pooling in the legs.
C) They reduce the risk of cardiac irregularities.
D) They increase the rate of lactic acid removal from the skeletal muscle.

66

Motor learning is when complex processes in the brain occur in response to practice or experience of a certain skill resulting in changes in the central nervous system that allows for the production of a new motor skill.

Which of the following stages of motor learning of the students is concerned with performing and refining the skills?

A) Cognitive stage
B) Associative stage
C) Dissociative stage
D) Autonomous stage

67

Which of the following actions best represents authentic assessment for a basketball skills unit?

A) Making a rubric to evaluate learners as they proceed through the unit
B) Using standardized instruments on basketball skills at the end of the unit
C) Keeping track of the number of baskets made in a class game
D) Using district-devised assessment of skills at the end of the game

68

Which of the following should a teacher initially provide in teaching a closed skill?

A) A changing environment with varying rates of skill performance

B) A changing environment with a constant rate of skill performance

C) A stable environment with varying rates of skill performance

D) A stable environment with a stable rate of skill performance

69

Equity is the quality of being fair and impartial.

In making an appropriate instruction for physical education, which of the following are the most critical core equity issues that a teacher must consider?

A) Values that are developed in sport activities

B) Learning objectives that are used when setting goals

C) Standards that are used to prepare the instruction

D) Individual differences in experience and skill levels, gender and cultural relevance

70

Educational Assessment is the systematic process of documenting and using empirical data on the knowledge, skill, attitudes, and beliefs to refine programs and improve student learning.

Which of the following should be ensured while doing careful planning for a physical education assessment?

A) Present in a formal written format which is familiar to students

B) Align with student outcomes and instructional frameworks

C) Develop based on students' comfortability and capability

D) Conjunction with the teacher's standard of evaluation

A hazard is any agent that can cause harm or damage to life, health, property or the environment.

In ensuring physical education facility to be free of hazards, which of the following is the most important procedure?

A) Ask students to use the facilities with care and not so often in order to avoid defects.

B) Attend seminars and conferences that involve specific case safety issues in different schools.

C) Make sure that safety inspections occur regularly and that resulting concerns are quickly addressed.

D) Compare physical education safety procedures to occupational safety standards and matching procedures to industry standards.

Educational measurement refers to the use of educational assessments and the analysis of data to infer the abilities and proficiencies of students.

Which of the following about the assessment is not true?

A) The most significant quality of a good assessment is validity.

B) While interpreting raw scores, knowledge of basic statistics is essential.

C) A standardized test is any form of test that requires all test takers to answer the same questions from a common bank of questions.

D) An assessment is a process of gathering information from multiple sources to understand what students know, understand, and can do with their knowledge.

73

Dance is a form of performing art consisting of purposefully selected sequences of human movement.

Which of the following styles of dance will be most appropriate to introduce to students that have mastery of fundamental skills for rhythmic movement?

A) Line dance
B) Modern dance
C) Ballroom dance
D) Contemporary dance

74

Which of the following will result in a flawless run of physical education in elementary schools?

A) Implementing strict rules for no interruptions during class.
B) Grouping students to lessen the load of program instruction.
C) Preparing the activity space and having the necessary equipment on hand prior to lesson activities.
D) Establishing and announcing to students time goals for each lesson activity

Throwing is the launching of a ballistic projectile by hand.

Which of the following should a physical education teacher do to improve the throwing skills of his students since most of them could not manage to use mature throwing patterns?

A) Prepare activities that highlight speed in throwing the ball.

B) Conduct lessons that emphasize throwing with varied effort.

C) Let them engage with students of other classes.

D) Let them observe students with good throwing skills.

Hereditary is a descriptive term for conditions capable of being transmitted from parent to offspring through the genes.

Which of the following areas of personal growth and development is the general contribution of heredity?

A) Body type and composition

B) Development of diseases acquired from stress

C) Level of physical strength towards training

D) Character quality towards building relationships

CONTINUE ▶

A physical education teacher notices that one of his students frequently appears drained and stated she has not received meals at home. The teacher is concerned that the student is being neglected.

Which of the following is the most appropriate action for the teacher to take about this student?

A) Talk to the student's previous teachers to determine if they observed similar signs of neglect.

B) Send home with the student a list of social service agencies that may be able to assist the family.

C) Contact the parents or guardians to express the student's concerns.

D) Report the suspected neglect in accordance with district guidelines.

Hopping is the movement with light bounding skips or leaps.

Which of the following would best explain that hopping will be more appropriate than skipping in introducing students to the rhythmic use of locomotor skills?

A) It requires minimal effort.

B) It is a controlled movement.

C) It involves one count and skipping involves two counts.

D) It moves in a different direction as compared to skipping.

CONTINUE ▶

79

A **modification** is a change or alteration, usually to make something work better.

Which of the following modifications would increase the success rate of all soccer players?

A) Widen the goal
B) Play in a larger field area
C) Have more players in the field
D) Increase the number of team members

80

Which of the following will have a bad result in contact sport wherein participants necessarily come into bodily contact with one another?

A) Enlarging field area dimensions
B) Assigning individual roles for each student
C) Forming teams in which one player is bigger, stronger, or more skilled than the other
D) Coaching students with different offensive and defensive styles

81

For research data to be of value and use, they must be both reliable and valid. **Reliability** refers to the repeatability of findings and **validity** refers to the credibility or believability of the research.

Which of the following defines validity?

A) The degree to which an assessment tool produces stable and consistent results
B) The extent to which a test accurately measures what it is supposed to measure
C) The extent to which an assessment measures the achievement of desired objectives
D) The extent to which an assessment covers all the items that have been taught or studied

CONTINUE ▶

Self-worth is the opinion you have about yourself and the value you place on yourself while self-esteem reflects a person's overall subjective emotional evaluation of his or her own worth.

A school has decided to conduct a field day with physical activities for students. One of the activities aim to hone student's self-esteem and sense of self-worth. Which of the following would be the most appropriate organizational approach?

A) Demonstrating activities that emphasize balance and speed

B) Creating more group activities than individual activities

C) Allowing students to activities based on their capabilities

D) Offering activities that allow students of varying fitness and skill levels to achieve individual success

Plyometrics is an exercise involving repeated rapid stretching and contracting of muscles, like in jumping and rebounding, to increase muscle power.

Which of the following is the purpose of plyometrics?

A) It is appropriate for explosive power training.

B) It is used to improve flexibility.

C) It is used for muscular endurance.

D) It is used for cardiovascular fitness.

A weekend athlete who exercises vigorously only on weekends, but not regularly during the week, does not exercise often enough to see solid results.

Which of the following principles of training does he violate?

A) The principle of progression
B) The principle of reversibility
C) The principle of rest and recovery
D) The principle of specificity of exercise

Which of the following is not included in the list of characteristics when performing a correct mature form of striking a ball with a racquet?

A) A person is coiling and rotating the body forward as the racquet is swung
B) A person is putting weight on the back foot and then shifting to the front foot as the racquet is swung
C) A person is stopping the racquet at the point of contact with the ball
D) A person is taking a forward step with the foot opposite to the striking arm

86

Milo was a six-time wrestling champion at the Ancient Olympic Games in Greece. It is believed that Milo lifted a newborn bull onto his shoulders each day until the bull became fully mature.

Which two principles of modern muscle strength and endurance conditioning did Milo follow?

A) Retention and Intensity

B) Overload and Progression

C) Progression and Frequency

D) Overload and Variable resistance

87

Muscle strength is the ability to exert a maximal amount of force for a short period of time while endurance training is the act of exercising to increase endurance.

Which of the following is the result of muscular strength and endurance training in the composition of the body?

A) Muscles atrophy as fat is reduced

B) Muscle mass increases with possible fat reduction

C) Muscle is enlarged due to fat accumulation

D) There is a high loss of weight due to fat elimination

Why is it essential for the physical education teacher to routinely check the first aid kit, batteries in the defibrillator, holes in the playing fields and other equipment as preparation for class?

A) To support school's vision and mission

B) To assist other staff members to fulfill their duty

C) To create s safe physical education learning environment

D) To implement the school's physical education curriculum

Which of the following is true while exerting maximum force on the ball at impact when swinging a tennis racket?

A) The speed of the strike should remain constant before impact with the ball.

B) The player should minimize extending his shoulder muscles as preparation for backswing.

C) The angular velocity of the swinging implement should be constant throughout.

D) The angular velocity of the swinging implement should be as big as possible.

Crawl is a swimming stroke in which arms are moved alternately overhead accompanied by a flutter kick.

Which of the following is the main reason of defining crawl as a continuous or repetitive motor task?

A) Recovery of the arms and legs leads directly into the next stroke, with no recognizable beginning and end

B) A variation of the front crawl where one arm always rests at the front while the other arm performs one cycle

C) Arms stay in the water and move synchronously while the legs perform a whip kick

D) Movement through the water can be sustained with no physical effort by keeping the body flat in the water

Which of the following is the advantage of a school-community collaboration that offers free services on local fitness facility to high school students that have undergone fitness instruction in class?

A) The collaboration allows students to manage their money management.

B) The collaboration allows students to divert from any detrimental factors and acquires less stress.

C) Previewing the facility improves chances that students will continue to use it, which benefits both the facility and students.

D) The collaboration allows physical education teachers to reallocate time usually spent on fitness to other instructional areas.

One important human function is the mobility, and the loss of it, or immobility may lead to many physical problems and emotional problems. It can also lead to detrimental cardiac, muscular, respiratory, skeletal, urinary, gastrointestinal, skin and emotional changes.

Which of the following is an example of a skeletal hazard of immobility?

A) Contractures
B) Constipation
C) Calcium loss
D) Catabolism

Strength training is a type of physical exercise specializing in the use of resistance to induce muscular contraction which builds the strength, anaerobic endurance, and size of skeletal muscles.

Which of the following should be the trainer's response to a female student that wants to do strength-training exercises without developing large muscles?

A) Training has a minimal effect on muscle strength for females since females tend to develop stronger bones.
B) Training develops large muscles on lower extremities for females due to shorter built.
C) Training promotes considerable gains in strength but only slight increases in muscle bulk because of females' low testosterone levels.
D) Toned muscles are necessary for gains in size and strength, so only females who begin training with well-defined muscles will develop larger ones.

94

Adolescence is the period of developmental transition between childhood and adulthood, involving multiple physical, intellectual, personality, and social developmental changes.

In the physical growth of infants and toddlers, which of the following is the typical development?

A) Physical growth occurs first in the head and proceeds downward to the trunk and outward toward the extremities.

B) Physical growth occurs in sudden changes in body shape and height.

C) Physical growth occurs variably in individuals with no typical starting point or progression of growth.

D) Physical growth co-occurs throughout the body.

95

Which of the following is the advantage of incorporating wellness technology programs in schools' physical education program?

A) Provide students and teachers with immediate access to data and allowing students to design, monitor and progress toward personal wellness goals.

B) Reduce time in manually demonstrating physical education lessons.

C) Establish a networking system by which physical education teachers can easily communicate with students' families, faculty, and service providers.

D) Allow students to evaluate their wellness and give information to their families in achieving better goals of awareness.

96

Stability is the ability of a substance to remain unchanged over time.

Which of the following could be the best explanation about stability, force and motion?

A) Size of the body is directly proportional to the force exerted.

B) People with large body have faster movement than people with smaller body segments.

C) Muscles with large cross-sectional areas can produce more force than smaller muscles.

D) A body's inertia, or resistance to change in a state of motion is proportional to body mass.

97

In secondary physical education programs, which of the following is a major challenge?

A) Providing adequate time and activities to encourage students to adopt a lasting ethic of physical activity

B) Providing activities that can be differentiated from middle school programs

C) Providing activities that would promote active and healthy lifestyle

D) Providing activities that each student can enjoy and appreciate

98

A motor disability is recognized as major when it causes significant and persistent limitations for the person in the course of his or her daily activities. Muscular or neurological systems responsible for body movement are affected, resulting in significant and persistent limitations in a person's daily life.

Which of the following should a teacher do to address a problem on a student with a motor disability who is having difficulty in providing enough force to pass a soccer ball?

A) Assign new lesson for the student

B) Transfer the student to another class

C) Shorten the student's length of activity

D) Force the student to embrace his limitations

99

A physical education teacher tells the student that he shoots the ball with proper hand position and suggests him to bend the knees more.

Which of the following is the teacher doing to improve the performance of the student?

A) He is instructing with simple terms.

B) He is setting another challenge for the student to go beyond his potential.

C) He is combining positive specific feedback with encouragement to correct one component of the skill

D) He is defining the motor task in visual terms for the student and providing spatial directions.

100

Muscular strength is the ability of a person to exert a force on physical objects using muscles. For the development of strength in arms, which of the following sets of exercises should be emphasized?

A) Front curls, bench presses, and shoulder shrugs

B) Front curls, bench presses, and tricep extensions

C) Front curls, overhead presses, and shoulder shrugs

D) Front curls, overhead presses, and tricep extensions

CONTINUE ▶

SECTION 1 - PHYSICAL EDUCATION

#	Answer	Topic	Subtopic	#	Answer	Topic	Subtopic	#	Answer	Topic	Subtopic	#	Answer	Topic	Subtopic
1	B	TB	S2	26	D	TB	S5	51	A	TB	S5	76	A	TB	S2
2	D	TB	S6	27	A	TB	S6	52	C	TB	S2	77	D	TB	S6
3	C	TB	S4	28	C	TB	S5	53	A	TB	S2	78	C	TB	S3
4	D	TB	S7	29	A	TB	S5	54	C	TB	S3	79	A	TB	S3
5	D	TB	S6	30	D	TB	S7	55	A	TB	S2	80	C	TB	S3
6	B	TB	S6	31	C	TB	S4	56	A	TB	S1	81	B	TB	S5
7	C	TB	S4	32	C	TB	S1	57	D	TB	S4	82	D	TB	S3
8	B	TB	S2	33	D	TB	S1	58	D	TB	S3	83	A	TB	S3
9	C	TB	S1	34	C	TB	S2	59	B	TB	S2	84	A	TB	S3
10	D	TB	S5	35	B	TB	S4	60	D	TB	S5	85	C	TB	S3
11	D	TB	S4	36	D	TB	S6	61	C	TB	S3	86	B	TB	S2
12	D	TB	S2	37	B	TB	S3	62	D	TB	S4	87	B	TB	S2
13	A	TB	S3	38	B	TB	S1	63	B	TB	S2	88	C	TB	S3
14	A	TB	S3	39	D	TB	S3	64	D	TB	S4	89	D	TB	S3
15	B	TB	S4	40	C	TB	S2	65	A	TB	S3	90	A	TB	S3
16	B	TB	S4	41	C	TB	S4	66	B	TB	S2	91	C	TB	S2
17	D	TB	S5	42	D	TB	S4	67	A	TB	S1	92	C	TB	S4
18	D	TB	S5	43	D	TB	S5	68	D	TB	S1	93	C	TB	S2
19	D	TB	S4	44	B	TB	S4	69	D	TB	S2	94	A	TB	S2
20	B	TB	S1	45	A	TB	S1	70	B	TB	S1	95	A	TB	S1
21	A	TB	S7	46	B	TB	S1	71	C	TB	S1	96	D	TB	S3
22	B	TB	S3	47	C	TB	S5	72	B	TB	S5	97	A	TB	S1
23	D	TB	S4	48	C	TB	S4	73	A	TB	S2	98	C	TB	S3
24	D	TB	S5	49	C	TB	S2	74	C	TB	S2	99	C	TB	S2
25	C	TB	S7	50	C	TB	S2	75	B	TB	S3	100	D	TB	S3

Topics & Subtopics

Code	Description	Code	Description
SB1	Planning Instruction	SB5	Student Assessment
SB2	Student Growth & Development	SB6	Communication, Collaboration & Technology
SB3	Planning Activities	SB7	Management & Motivation
SB4	Health-Related Physical Fitness	TB	Physical Education

CONTINUE ▶

TEST DIRECTION

DIRECTIONS

Read the questions carefully and then choose the ONE best answer to each question.

Be sure to allocate your time carefully so you are able to complete the entire test within the testing session. You may go back and review your answers at any time.

You may use any available space in your test booklet for scratch work.

Questions in this booklet are not actual test questions but they are the samples for commonly asked questions.

This test aims to cover all topics which may appear on the actual test. However some topics may not be covered.

Studying this booklet will be preparing you for the actual test. It will not guarantee improving your test score but it will help you pass your exam on the first attempt.

Some useful tips for answering multiple choice questions;

- Start with the questions that you can easily answer.

- Underline the keywords in the question.

- Be sure to read all the choices given.

- Watch for keywords such as NOT, always, only, all, never, completely.

- Do not forget to answer every question.

 CONTINUE ▶

When attempting to control a wound from bleeding, which of the following methods should be used first?

A) Making a tourniquet and putting it on the wound.

B) Applying pressure to the cut and elevating the bleeding portion.

C) Utilizing an air splint to form a pressure bandage.

D) Placing pressure indirectly to the wound by putting the thumb on the pressure area.

Which of the following diseases is considered one of the most common sexually transmitted infections in the United States and is very serious since it usually shows no symptoms until subsequent damage occurs?

A) Syphilis: A sexually transmitted disease (STD), bacterial infection, caused by bacteria

B) Herpes simplex: An infection that is caused by a herpes simplex virus (HSV)

C) Chlamydia: A sexually transmitted disease (STD) which is easily spread because it often causes no symptoms

D) Gonorrhea: A sexually transmitted disease (STD) that can affect the female reproductive tract and vagina.

U.S. FOOD & DRUG
ADMINISTRATION

Food and Drug Administration, or FDA, is a federal agency that is responsible for protecting and improving public health. It requires U.S. food corporations to include additives in specific food products, such as folate in grain products and iodine in salt.

Which of the following is a primary objective of these types of policies?

A) To decrease the need for adding food preservatives food to limit spoilage.

B) To assure that Americans get the needed daily intake of all vital micronutrients.

C) To counterbalance the food proteins that induce allergic reactions to some people and produce antibodies.

D) To reduce the health risks associated with nutrient deficiencies such as cardiovascular problems and congenital disabilities.

A child's growth and development, as well as energy needs, can be fulfilled by which of the following dietary patterns?

A) Eating carbohydrate-rich foods to counter any change in blood sugar levels.

B) Avoiding foods containing fats to prevent problems with vitamin and mineral absorption.

C) Eating small meals for the day which consists of carbohydrates, fats, proteins, vitamins, minerals, and water for the day.

D) Consuming a large, well-balanced meal throughout the day for the energy needs during the day's activities and comfortable sleep at night.

CONTINUE ▶

5

Type II Herpes, or genital herpes, is an infection caused by the herpes simplex virus II (HSV-II) and is generally transmitted through sexual contact.

This disease is characterized by which of the following?

A) Burning sensation when peeing
B) Clumps of tiny blisters around the genitals
C) White pus-like secretion and discomfort during sexual intercourse
D) Pink to red cauliflower-shaped masses in or around the sex organ

6

Check on the victim and do not move him unless necessary. If the person shows no signs of life, such as breathing, coughing or movement then you can begin CPR.

In which of the following positions a shock victim should be placed before giving first aid?

A) In a semi-sitting position
B) On his back with the legs elevated
C) On his back with the head elevated
D) In the recovery position, on his side

7

Defibrillation is a method used in medicine to stop ventricular fibrillation or pulseless ventricular tachycardia. It utilizes an electric shock to allow the restoration of the heart's normal rhythm.

Which of the following factors should be ensured first before doing automated external defibrillation on a heart attack victim?

A) There must be an ambulance nearby.
B) The victim's arms should be in a secured position.
C) No one must be in direct contact with the victim.
D) There must be sufficient inclination to the victim's head.

8

Alateen is a fellowship program for teenagers, whose lives have been affected by someone else's drinking.

Which of the following is the primary goal of the organization called Alateen?

A) Providing social support to teenagers affected by alcoholism in their families.
B) Developing alcohol recovery programs for teenagers.
C) Funding public high schools for their alcohol prevention programs.
D) Establishing partnerships with public agencies in communities to cope with alcoholism.

CONTINUE ▶

9

Vitamin K molecules consists of structurally similar, fat-soluble vitamins such as phylloquinone (Vitamin K1), menaquinone (Vitamin K2), and menadione (Vitamin K3). It is found mainly in green leaves.

Which of the following is the importance of Vitamin K in the human body?

A) It is vital for blood clotting.

B) It is needed for bone formation.

C) It is crucial for the absorption of minerals.

D) It is needed for maintaining the good condition of the skin tissues.

10

What is the primary goal of food biotechnology?

A) To develop foods for space explorations

B) To improve the health and safety of foods

C) To clone agricultural products such as tomatoes

D) To increase the productions of milk, meat, and other agricultural products

11

Incomplete proteins lack in one or more amino acids that are important in building cells.

Which of the following is not a dietary source of an incomplete protein?

A) Eggs

B) Nuts

C) Grains

D) Legumes

12

All organized private and public measures aiming to prevent disease, promote health and prolong life among the population as a whole refers to Public Health.

Which of the following is not one of the core functions of public health?

A) Assessment, Policy development, and Assurance are three main functions of public health.

B) Assurance refers informing, educating and empowering the community.

C) Assessment refers monitoring health, diagnosing and investigating health problems.

D) Policy development refers improving the use of scientific knowledge to improve the communities health.

There are three distinct types of muscles in the human body; skeletal, cardiac, and smooth. Each type of muscle tissue has a unique structure and a specific role. Skeletal muscle moves bones and other structures, the Cardiac muscle contracts the heart to pump blood, the smooth muscle tissue forms organs like the stomach and changes shape to facilitate body functions.

Which of the following muscles in the human body function voluntarily?

A) Smooth
B) Cardiac
C) Sarcomere
D) Skeletal

Public Health prevents epidemics and the spread of disease, protects against environmental hazards, prevents injuries, promotes and encourages healthy behaviors, responds to disasters and assists communities in recovery, assures the quality and accessibility of health services.

Which of the following about the diseases is not correct?

A) Tuberculosis (TB) is primarily an airborne disease which is spread person -to-person through the air.
B) Obesity, Type 2 diabetes and Cardiovascular diseases are related to over-nutrition
C) Chlamydia is a sexually transmitted diseases which has the lowest incidence in the United States.
D) Cholera is an infectious disease caused by a bacterium resulting in severe diarrhea and dehydration that can result in death; was thought to be caused by miasma.

## 15

One of the symptoms of having an eating disorder is having abnormal or disturbed eating habit like anorexia nervosa.

Which of the following is considered first if a student has an eating disorder?

A) Monitor the food intake
B) Check the weight regularly
C) Refer the student to the doctor
D) Make sure to have a balanced diet in place

The government conducts various prevention programs regarding substance abuse.

Among these programs aimed at preventing substance abuse, which of the following is the least effective?

A) Life-skills training
B) Value clarification
C) Teaching how to develop self-esteem
D) Teaching awareness about the effects of substance abuse.

## 17

Many programs or activities are made to reduce alcoholism as well as the drug abuse within a community.

Which of the following actions would have the least effect on controlling alcoholism and drug abuse?

A) Increasing the number of law enforcers near the schools.
B) Putting high taxes on tobacco products and alcoholic beverages.
C) Limiting the number of bars within a community by having zoning ordinances.
D) Implementing drug prevention programs with the parents and students as the target audience.

Which of the following elements in the hemoglobin, a protein found in red blood cells, is responsible for binding oxygen?

A) Iron
B) Calcium
C) Phosphorus
D) Magnesium

19

Anxiety refers to persistent and excessive feelings of tension, nervousness, anxious thoughts about many different things.

Anxiety is a very normal response to stressful life events, but when it becomes more substantial, then it interferes with your life and can cause serious mental health problems.

Which of the following about anxiety is not correct?

A) Anxiety causes the body to feel fatigue, restlessness, or sweating.

B) Lack of concentration, racing thoughts, or unwanted thoughts is the cognitive symptoms of anxiety.

C) Anxiety disorders are among the most common mental disorders in the United States.

D) It's possible to develop generalized anxiety disorder as an adult, but children do not exhibit anxiety.

20

Gina has an average daily intake of 175g of protein, 350g of carbohydrate, and 100g of fat. What percent of Gina's total calorie intake is protein?

A) 23.3%

B) 28%

C) 30.2%

D) 45%

21

Immunization is a very important primary prevention. It is the ability of an organism to resist a specific infection by the specific antibodies or white blood cells.

Which of the following about immunity is not correct?

A) Human immune system produces antibodies specifically to fight a particular invading substance.

B) Breast feeding is very important for an infant because antibodies in breast milk allow the passive transfer of immunity from mother to baby.

C) AIDS (acquired immunodeficiency syndrome) is caused by the human immunodeficiency virus (HIV) in which the immune system is too weak to fight off infection.

D) Immunity acquired after an infection is called as innate immunity and passive immunity is obtained through injection of antibodies.

22

Which of the following statements best describes the reason why daily dental flossing is highly recommended?

A) Dental flossing prevents bad breath.

B) Dental flossing prevents formation of plaque.

C) It is crucial in maintaining the space between the teeth to avoid crowding of the teeth.

D) It helps removing the food particles trapped in between the teeth which may result in tooth decay.

23

Which of the following defines HAACP?

A) An agency in the government that controls the price of goods in the market

B) A list of guidelines for training employees in the food industry

C) A list of guidelines for ensuring food safety in processing, packaging, distribution, storage, and preparation

D) The agency in the government that inspects the labeling in commercial products

24

Which of the following explains why the Physicians' Desk Reference (PDR) Consumer Drug Information online database is regularly consulted?

A) To investigate marketing methods and to promote newly registered drugs.

B) To collect data on the prices imposed by local drugs stores.

C) To collect information on proper dosages, side effects, and potential interactions of specific drugs.

D) To find the lists of drugs approved and covered by particular health insurance policies.

47

CONTINUE ▶

25

The **brain** is an organ that acts as the central nervous system. Some of its primary function are the processing of information and releasing hormones. A specific part of the brain is responsible for determining the reaction of the body to stress and acts as the sympathetic nervous system's control center.

Which of the following parts of the brain is responsible for the functions mentioned above?

A) Cerebellum
B) Hypothalamus
C) Corpus callosum
D) Prefrontal cortex

26

Headache is pain that may occur on one or both sides of the head and it affects the quality of life.

Which of the following is associated with stress-related headaches?

A) The level of glucose in the bloodstream is decreased.
B) The blood vessels that lead to the brain is constricting.
C) The muscles on the neck as well as the back of the head are experiencing sustained contractions.
D) Eating foods such as nuts and chocolates cause a reaction due to proteins present on them.

CONTINUE ▶

27

Which of the following websites would help a community member most in searching the advantages and disadvantages of major health plans, prescription plans, and prevention and wellness programs?

A) AHRQ; Agency for Healthcare Research and Quality
B) WHO; World Health Organization
C) CDC; Centers for Disease Control and Prevention
D) OSHA; Occupational Safety and Health Administration

28

Some common **pathogens** are viruses, bacteria, fungi, protozoa, and worms.

Which of the following about a pathogen is correct?

A) It is necessary for body function.
B) It is anything that can cause disease.
C) It can be seen without a microscope.
D) It is a kind of protein which produces antibodies.

29

Diet, physical fitness, and individual health are interrelated with each other.

To better enhance a student's understanding of it, which of the following nutritional tools would most likely be useful?

A) The nutritional fact sheets for each major food group.
B) Understanding the relationship between nutrition and disease risk factors by reading medical journal articles.
C) Software programs capable of considering personal profiles to analyze food intake and activity levels.
D) The nutritional values of foods as well as the calories lost by different physical activities listed on appendixes and tables.

30

Some psychosocial disorders may develop or first become apparent during adolescence.

Which of the following psychosocial problems are more common among girls during adolescence?

A) Mood disorders
B) Eating disorders
C) Antisocial behavior
D) Lack of self control

31

Maggie's blood test result shows that she has a high cholesterol level. Her doctor Nicole gives Maggie some advice about the ways to lower her cholesterol.

Considering that Maggie has a partner, by which of the following ways can her partner influence her effectively for a healthy lifestyle?

A) Give Maggie a gym membership and encourage her to work out regularly.

B) Give Maggie self-help nutritional books from the library.

C) To obtain high accuracy for the next test on the follow-up check-up, Maggie's partner needs to ensure that she fasts before having the test.

D) Show support to Maggie's new healthy lifestyle instructed by her doctor by also doing what Maggie is doing such as eating low-fat, high-fiber meals each day.

32

A teacher wants to improve his student's motivation and feelings of academic success.

Which of the following approaches would be the most effective in achieving this goal and helping students develop self-esteem?

A) Reporting student's achievement to the parents and guardians

B) Helping students in developing their goals based on their strengths and needs

C) Making a list of learning objectives for all students based on their weak areas

D) Giving the students an opportunity to share the benefits of their learning objectives with their friends

33

Which of the following shows the conflict associated with globalization considering the current issue of an international traveler with resistant TB?

A) Lack of international centers for disease control.

B) Differences between global healthcare management.

C) Insufficient international health insurance plan.

D) The danger of spreading of dangerous pathogens as well as contagious disease.

34

Which of the following best describes the importance of the ozone layer in the upper atmosphere?

A) Enhancement of the greenhouse effect

B) The ozone layer absorbs harmful ultraviolet radiation.

C) It is responsible for the increase in all types of skin cancer.

D) It leads to a reduction on the amount of acid rain as well as urban smog.

35

Depression is a common and serious medical illness which is characterized as a mood disorder that causes a persistent feeling of sadness and loss of interest for long periods of time.

Which of the following is the most common symptom of depression?

A) High anxiety in daily life activities.

B) Extreme fears that are not realistic.

C) Eating too much and sleeping too much.

D) Loss of interest and pleasure in ordinary activities including sex.

36

Mary used to take on too many tasks and activities. However recently, she is refusing to participate new activities.

Which of the following is Mary exhibiting?

A) Laziness

B) Multitasking

C) Procrastination

D) Time management

Cancer is defined as the group of diseases that involves the abnormal growth of cells with the ability to migrate and spread to other parts of the body.

Which of the following options best illustrates the three general warning indications of cancer?

A) Abnormal bleeding, unhealed sores, and the appearance of lumps on the body

B) Extreme headaches, light sensitivity, and development of cataract

C) Weight loss, weakness and exhaustion, and swelling of the joints

D) Nausea and vomiting, severe muscle spasms, and pressure in the chest

Alexa is bothered by her daughter's mental health since she has been showing signs of withdrawal and depression. She schedules a doctor appointment.

In this situation, which of the following additional actions is most significant for Alexa to take?

A) Spend a long weekend trip to provide a change of pace and scenery for her daughter.

B) Strive to involve her daughter in a talking therapy wherein the mother assumes the position of a mental health counselor.

C) Study and search for therapy alternatives associated with teenage depression on the Internet to prepare for various diagnoses.

D) Show her support, have constant communication with her, and observe for any bothersome behavior.

39

_____ pressure is required to be generated within the thoracic cavity in order for the diaphragm to contract. In this condition, the lungs would tend to _____.

Which of the following terms correctly complete the statements given above?

A) Negative, Expand
B) Positive, Expand
C) Positive, Contract
D) Negative, Contract

40

Epidemiology is the study of the distribution and determinants of health-related events, and the control of diseases and other health problems.

Which of the following about epidemiology is not correct?

A) Louis Pasteur is the father of medicine who introduced the term "epidemic"
B) Pandemic is the epidemic affecting a large number of people, many countries, continents, or regions worldwide.
C) Epidemiologists generally use the incidence rate to refer to the number of new cases of a disease in a population within a specified time period.
D) John Snow is the father of epidemiology who provided an example of both analytic and descriptive epidemiological study.

The word "**vitamin**" was derived from the word "vitamine" that was coined in 1911 by the biochemist Casimir Funk (1884-1967). Vitamins are essential for regular growth and development of an organism. Vitamins must be consumed periodically and in a limited amount to avoid deficiency.

Which of the following about the vitamins is not correct?

A) Your body can also make vitamins D and K but if you have a vegetarian diet you may need to take a vitamin B12 supplement because it is found in foods such as meat, fish, and dairy products.

B) Vitamin K is found naturally in vegetables, beans, eggs, strawberries and meat, and deficiency of Vitamin K can cause the risk of uncontrolled bleeding.

C) Water soluble vitamins (vitamin B and C) have to be taken in the diet more frequently than fat soluble vitamins.

D) Vitamin D (sometimes called the as the sunshine vitamin) is produced by the action of ultraviolet rays on the skin and the deficiency of Vitamin D is not widespread in US.

When drinking water is contaminated with nitrate it is transformed to nitrite in the digestive system. The nitrite oxidizes the iron in the hemoglobin of the red blood cells and forms methemoglobin, which decreases the oxygen-carrying ability of hemoglobin.

Which of the following sources of pollution can be controlled to reduce the high levels of nitrites and nitrates in drinking water?

A) Septic systems of the buildings

B) Agricultural runoff originating from the fields and feedlots

C) Wastewater discharged by heavy industry

D) Treated wastewater released by the municipal sewage-treatment plants

43

Cardiovascular disease refers to diseases involving the heart or blood vessel particularly, a narrowed or blocked blood vessel which may result in complications such as heart attack. Adolescents, in particular, are advised to take active steps to avoid having cardiovascular disease.

Which of the following best describes why the adolescents are given advice?

A) The risk of developing cardiovascular disease is greatly influenced by things done during adolescence.

B) Using standard diagnostic tools for detecting cardiovascular disease is not effective in adolescents.

C) The risk factors for adolescents are prevalent as compared with other age groups.

D) Treating cardiovascular disease in adolescents and young adults are hard to manage and control.

44

Fiber absorbs water on its way through the digestive systems and results in a softer stool. Because of this property of fiber, eating fiber-rich foods reduces the risk of which of the following?

A) Hypertension

B) Hemorrhoids

C) Heart disease

D) Osteoporosis

45

Which of the following statements best describes the American Red Cross?

A) It is a non-profit health foundation that aims to the enhance health.

B) It is an organization that aims to assist in emergency and disaster relief.

C) It is a health association that aims to improve the national health information services.

D) It is an organization that aims to protect the consumers in the health-care marketplace.

46

A patient caught a bacterial infection. He has a high fever and has been experiencing chest pains, persistent cough, chills, and fluid accumulation.

The early stages of this disease would be most receptive in which of the following types of treatment?

A) Antibiotics

B) Vaccinations

C) Cortisone shots

D) Vitamin supplements

47

Which of the following describes the behaviors of an adolescent who displays a consistent depressive mood and significant susceptibility to stress?

A) Normal feelings which are expected for adolescents.

B) Hormonal changes associated with puberty resulting in these behaviors.

C) Personal risk factors which are associated with substance abuse.

D) Risk factors which are associated with participation in a deviant subculture.

48

Most people worldwide are immediately affected by which of the following environmental issues?

A) Air pollution

B) Land pollution

C) Water pollution

D) Noise pollution

49

Which of the following mental disorder is most frequently diagnosed in the United States?

A) Eating disorder which is characterized by abnormal or disturbed eating habits.

B) Anxiety disorder which means having regular or uncontrollable worries about many different things in your everyday life.

C) Mood disorder which is a psychological disorder characterized by the elevation or lowering of a person's mood.

D) Substance abuse which means being dependent on an addictive substance, especially alcohol or drugs.

50

• Population movement
• Transport of pathogens across borders
• The resistance of pathogens to antibiotics
• Technological variations related to the mass production of food

The details given above best illustrates the factors affecting which of the following?

A) Treatment of infectious illnesses

B) Transmission of degenerative diseases

C) Incidence and prevalence of developing diseases

D) Diagnosis and control of long-term diseases

51

Amniocentesis is a medical procedure that involves getting a sample of the amniotic fluid, which contains cells from the fetus, and will be subjected for analysis. It is typically performed between 14 and 20 weeks.

Which of the following is amniocentesis often used for?

A) Facilitating artificial insemination
B) Determining if there are certain disabilities present on a fetus
C) Estimating the potential of a woman to handle pregnancy to a term
D) Measuring the capability of transplant recipients in terms of immune response

52

Minerals are substances that occur naturally on Earth.

Which of the following is an example of minerals?

A) Iron
B) Sunlight
C) Vitamin D
D) Vitamin B12

53

In order to have the occupational risks of workers monitored, the U.S government commonly uses which of the following public health strategy?

A) Health facilities and laboratories are required to report occupational lung diseases, poisoning due to pesticide and metal, and radiation illness.
B) Training programs on hazardous substances like asbestos worker training and certification programs are conducted.
C) Anecdotal information and case studies that are reported by individual workers to the public health departments are collected.
D) The indoor and outdoor air quality and drinking water supplies are tested regularly in major urban areas of the United States.

54

Which of the following order of the female reproductive parts shows the sperm's pathway towards the site of fertilization?

A) Vagina, Cervix, Fallopian tube, Uterus
B) Vagina, Cervix, Uterus, Fallopian tube
C) Vagina, Uterus, Fallopian tube, Cervix
D) Urethra, Vagina, Fallopian tube, Uterus

CONTINUE ▶

55

Which of the following elements helps to maintain normal nerve and muscle function, supports a healthy immune system, keeps the heartbeat steady, and helps bones remain strong?

A) Iron

B) Sodium

C) Potassium

D) Magnesium

56

Pneumonia is a disease caused by bacteria and viruses in one or both lungs. This infection causes difficulty in breathing due to which of the following?

A) Loss of elasticity of the alveoli

B) Filling of the lungs with fluid

C) Tissue breakdown in the lungs

D) Swelling of the bronchial passages

57

Body organs perform specific actions in the human body.

The discharge of liquid wastes in the body is the primary function of which of the following organs?

A) Skin

B) Lungs

C) Kidneys

D) Small Intestine

58

Which of the following U.S. government agencies regulate the use of food additives?

A) Food and Drug Administration

B) Department of Health and Human Services

C) United States Department of Agriculture

D) United States Department of Trade and Industry

CONTINUE ▶

There are different Government Agencies involved in Health Issues. Which of the following about the golas of these agencies is not correct?

A) Environmental Protection Agency (EPA) examines environmental health issues and makes recommendations.

B) Department of Agriculture & the FDA protects the nation's food supply.

C) Department of Homeland Security sets radiation safety standards for nuclear power plants and other sources of energy.

D) Occupational Safety and Health Administration (OSHA) aims to reduce injuries and hazardous exposures in the workplace

A **divorce** between two people can cause emotional stress, especially in children. During the time that the family structure is changing, which of the following approaches can effectively help the children handle this stressor?

A) Transferring to a new neighborhood to make a new start

B) Keeping a stable routine at home and in school

C) Spending more time with family and friends

D) Reading and consulting books about family life

Which of the following would a 15-year-old girl most likely feel if she had trouble making friends in her new school?

A) Proud

B) Excited

C) Socially inadequate

D) Glad she left her old school

Public Health means Prevent, Promote and Protect. The goal of public health is to prevent disease and disability.

Which of the following about public health is not correct?

A) Government, health care professionals, and community members are responsible for public health.

B) If necessary to protect the health of the public, a public health officer may confine an individual to detention or prison.

C) A principle of public health is that the health of the individual is not tied to his/her community.

D) Preventing epidemics and injuries, protecting against environmental hazards, and promoting healthy behaviors are some of the purposes of public health.

63

Hemophilia is a disorder wherein the blood cannot clot properly and may lead to continuous bleeding. **Sickle-cell disease**, on the other hand, is a blood disorder that affects hemoglobin.

These diseases can be used to show the relationship between which of the following?

A) Aging and the development of persistent diseases

B) Lifestyle practices and the growth of disease

C) Environmental factors and the progress of chronic disease

D) Hereditary factors and the evolution of disease

64

Which of the following information does Health History Questionnaire collect?

A) Evidence of disclosure

B) Previous exercise history

C) Fitness measurement data

D) Detailed medical report form doctor

65

Secondary prevention's goal is to reduce the progression of disease or any health related issue that an individual already has and does not know it.

Which of the following information about secondary prevention is not correct?

A) Secondary prevention is done by treating disease or injury as soon as possible to stop or slow its progress.

B) Implementing chronic disease management and rehabilitation programs are examples of secondary prevention.

C) Daily diet and exercise programs to prevent further heart attacks or strokes are examples of secondary prevention.

D) Regular screening tests to identify disease in its earliest stages like breast cancer screening are examples of secondary prevention.

66

Its mission is to ensure that employees work in a safe and healthful environment by setting and enforcing standards.

Which of the following U.S federal government agencies is responsible for the establishment and implementation of standards mentioned above?

A) National Institutes of Health

B) National Labor Relation Board

C) Occupational Safety and Health Administration

D) Center for Disease and Control Prevention

67

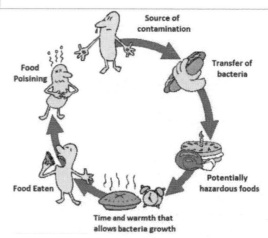

Food contamination is a common problem when mishandling food during food preparation and may cause health problems to consumers. To prevent food contamination, there are rules set to be followed strictly.

Which of the following is the most important food preparation and storage practice followed to prevent food contamination?

A) During food preparation, always use a porous wood cutting board.

B) Avoid eating leftover foods stored in the refrigerator for more than two days.

C) Do not put raw meat and seafood alongside other foods when preparing.

D) The eggs, milk, and cheese or any dairy product should be placed in the coldest parts of the refrigerator.

Drugs are substances that exhibit a physiological effect when ingested or introduced to the body.

Which of the following drug types can most possibly create physical dependence when used?

A) Barbiturates: Drugs that act as a central nervous system depressant

B) Inhalants: Medicinal preparations that produce chemical vapors for inhaling.

C) Steroids: Drugs used to relieve swelling and inflammation, such as prednisone and cortisone

D) Hallucinogens: Drugs that alter perception (awareness of surrounding objects and conditions), thoughts, and feelings.

The constant exposure of humans or other organisms to high sound levels which may result in adverse effects is referred to as **noise pollution**.

Which of the following health problems will most likely result from noise pollution?

A) Chemical hypersensitivities

B) Illnesses that are stress-related

C) Dizziness and visual disorders

D) Obsessive compulsive disorders (OCD)

70

Hormones have several functions in the human body. Which hormone is responsible for reducing inflammation and known as "stress hormone"?

A) Insulin

B) Cortisol

C) Testosterone

D) Growth hormone

71

After aerobic training and resistance training, how does the density of mitochondria change?

A) For both trainings it increases

B) For both trainings it decreases

C) After aerobic training it increases and after resistance training it decreases

D) After aerobic training it decreases and after resistance training it increases

72

What do we call the sudden relaxation of muscle after experienceing high tension?

A) Muscle inhibition

B) Reciprocal inhibition

C) Mechanoreceptor

D) Autogenic inhibition

73

By which of the following are the muscle fiber receptors at the neuromuscular junction stimulated?

A) Calcium ions

B) Acetylcholine

C) Creatine phosphate

D) Adenosine triphosphate (ATP)

Who among the persons listed below is prone to heart disease?

A) Ben, a 32 year-old man with 130/70 mmHg

B) Jonas, a 37 year-old man with 140/90 mmHg

C) James, a 38 year-old man with 121/81 mmHg

D) Sheena, an 18 year-old girl with 120/80 mmHg

Absolute strength is the maximal force that a person can exert no matter how big or small is a person's muscle or body.

Which of the following statements about absolute strength is true?

A) Generally, women have about one third the strength of men.

B) Women can exert the same amount of strength as men.

C) Generally, women have about half the strength of men.

D) Generally, women have about two thirds the strength of men.

Anabolism, constructive metabolism, is the synthesis of complex molecules in living organisms from simpler ones together with the storage of energy.

Which of the following is an example of anabolism?

A) Forming of proteins from amino acids

B) The disintegration of carbohydrates into glucose

C) Forming of small molecules from large molecules

D) Disintegration of large molecules into smaller molecules

Which of the following refers to the state of physical, emotional, intellectual, and spiritual depletion characterized by feelings of helplessness and hopelessness?

A) Fatigue

B) Burnout

C) Negativeness

D) Traumatization

78

Which of the following is not the function of the cardiovascular system in the human body?

A) To oxygenate the blood through gas exchange.

B) To transport nutrients, gases and waste products around the body.

C) To protect the body from infection and blood loss.

D) To help the body maintain constant body temperature (thermoregulation)

79

The physical activity of low to high intensity that is dependent on the aerobic energy-generating process is called **aerobic exercise**. Breathing and heart rate increases during an aerobic exercise session so that blood containing oxygen is distributed to the working muscle.

What factor is increased so that it causes the stimulation of pumping of blood during aerobic exercise?

A) Hemoglobin

B) Cardiac output

C) Blood glucose

D) Plasma volume

80

Antibiotics are medicines used to treat a wide variety of infections or diseases caused by bacteria, such as respiratory tract infections, urinary tract infections, skin infections and infected wounds. Antibiotics have had both positive and negative impacts on society.

Which of the following can be considered as a negative impact of antibiotics?

A) New types of cancers have developed due to extensive use of antibiotics.

B) Over-abundance of medical professionals.

C) Increased obesity in humans due to use in consumer products.

D) Resistant strains of bacteria caused by extensive use of antibiotics.

81

Which of the following is correct about anxiety?

A) Most antidepressant drugs can treat anxiety disorders.

B) The person can perform at his best when he is anxious and fearful.

C) Most people diagnosed with anxiety disorders have less activity in the fear circuit of their brains.

D) Most people diagnosed with anxiety disorders can live normal lives without treatment.

The number associated with a specific type of food that indicates the food's effect on a person's blood sugar level is called the **glycemic index**.

After an exercise session of Paul, which of the following food should he consume for the highest glycemic index to replenish glycogen stores?

A) Yogurt

B) Green beans

C) Orange juice

D) Mashed potatoes

83

Mood disorders is a group of mental conditions that is mainly caused by disturbances in an individual's mood.

Which of the following gives the two common types of mood disorders?

A) Bipolar and tripolar disorders

B) Bipolar and unipolar disorders

C) Schizophrenia and depression

D) Biological and psychosocial disorders

What is the condition in which an excess of interstitial fluid would lead to swelling of the tissue?

A) Edema

B) Eczema

C) Hydration

D) Dehydration

SECTION 2 - GENERAL HEALTH

#	Answer	Topic	Subtopic	#	Answer	Topic	Subtopic	#	Answer	Topic	Subtopic	#	Answer	Topic	Subtopic
1	B	TC	S7	22	B	TC	S1	43	A	TC	S1	64	D	TC	S3
2	C	TC	S7	23	C	TC	S4	44	B	TC	S4	65	B	TC	S3
3	D	TC	S7	24	C	TC	S7	45	B	TC	S3	66	C	TC	S5
4	C	TC	S4	25	B	TC	S6	46	A	TC	S7	67	C	TC	S4
5	B	TC	S7	26	C	TC	S1	47	C	TC	S2	68	A	TC	S7
6	B	TC	S7	27	A	TC	S3	48	C	TC	S5	69	B	TC	S5
7	C	TC	S7	28	B	TC	S4	49	B	TC	S2	70	B	TC	S6
8	A	TC	S3	29	C	TC	S4	50	C	TC	S7	71	C	TC	S6
9	A	TC	S4	30	B	TC	S1	51	B	TC	S6	72	D	TC	S6
10	A	TC	S4	31	D	TC	S4	52	A	TC	S4	73	B	TC	S6
11	A	TC	S4	32	B	TC	S2	53	A	TC	S3	74	B	TC	S7
12	B	TC	S3	33	D	TC	S3	54	B	TC	S6	75	D	TC	S6
13	D	TC	S6	34	B	TC	S5	55	D	TC	S6	76	A	TC	S6
14	C	TC	S3	35	D	TC	S2	56	B	TC	S7	77	B	TC	S2
15	C	TC	S4	36	D	TC	S1	57	C	TC	S6	78	A	TC	S6
16	D	TC	S4	37	A	TC	S7	58	A	TC	S4	79	B	TC	S6
17	A	TC	S3	38	D	TC	S2	59	C	TC	S3	80	D	TC	S7
18	A	TC	S4	39	C	TC	S6	60	B	TC	S2	81	A	TC	S2
19	D	TC	S2	40	D	TC	S3	61	C	TC	S2	82	D	TC	S4
20	B	TC	S4	41	D	TC	S4	62	C	TC	S3	83	B	TC	S2
21	D	TC	S3	42	B	TC	S5	63	D	TC	S7	84	A	TC	S7

Topics & Subtopics

Code	Description	Code	Description
SC1	Personal Health	SC5	Environmental Health
SC2	Mental & Emotional Health	SC6	Anatomy & Physiology
SC3	Community Health	SC7	Health Promotion & Prevention of Injury and Diseases
SC4	Nutrition Health	TC	General Health

CONTINUE ▶

TEST DIRECTION

DIRECTIONS

Read the questions carefully and then choose the ONE best answer to each question.

Be sure to allocate your time carefully so you are able to complete the entire test within the testing session. You may go back and review your answers at any time.

You may use any available space in your test booklet for scratch work.

Questions in this booklet are not actual test questions but they are the samples for commonly asked questions.

This test aims to cover all topics which may appear on the actual test. However some topics may not be covered.

Studying this booklet will be preparing you for the actual test. It will not guarantee improving your test score but it will help you pass your exam on the first attempt.

Some useful tips for answering multiple choice questions;

- Start with the questions that you can easily answer.

- Underline the keywords in the question.

- Be sure to read all the choices given.

- Watch for keywords such as NOT, always, only, all, never, completely.

- Do not forget to answer every question.

1

Cooling down is an easy exercise, done after more intense activity, to allow the body to gradually rest.

Which of the following about cooling down is not correct?

A) It allows the heart rate to return to its resting rate.

B) A simple and effective means of cooling down is to continue to exercise at a slower pace.

C) It provides the body with a quick transition from exercise back to a steady state of rest.

D) Cooling down after physical activity is important because it prevents muscle soreness.

2

Endurance is the ability of an organism to remain active for a long period of time. **Muscular endurance** is the ability of a muscle or group of muscles to sustain repeated contractions against a resistance for a long period of time. It is one of the components of muscular fitness, along with muscular strength and power.

Which of the following about muscular endurance is not correct?

A) Muscular endurance is not related to a person's muscular strength.

B) Improving your muscular endurance can make everyday activities easier.

C) The combination of strength and endurance results in muscular endurance.

D) To be able to run quickly over a short distance is an example of muscular endurance.

3

Physical education started in the United States in 1820 wherein immigrants influenced schools on activities such gymnastics and care and development of the human body.

Which of the following is one of the origin country of immigrants that greatly influence the early development of P.E. in the United States?

A) China

B) Russia

C) Germany

D) Switzerland

4

Swimming is a full-body sport that requires intensive training. The goal of the swimmer is to reach a specified distance in the shortest time possible or with the lowest number of strokes possible.

Which of the following health-related skill is not improved by swimming?

A) Flexibility

B) Foot speed

C) Muscle endurance

D) Cardio-respiratory function

5

Amateur sports refer to sports in which participants engage primarily without remuneration.

Which of the following professional organizations protects amateur sports from corruption?

A) NBA

B) AAU

C) AAPI

D) AAHPERD

6

Protein is one of the essential components of building one's muscles. Consumed protein can be transformed for the muscle's use upon proper exercise.

Which of the following is true for the protein content of an animal?

A) It is a complete protein

B) It is a fragmented protein

C) It is a non-essential protein

D) It is an incomplete protein

CONTINUE ▶

7

Injuries are common in physical activities, even when taking the utmost precaution during the activities.

Which of the following is a legal error that results in a direct or indirect injury?

A) A Tort
B) Negligence
C) Legal liability
D) In loco parentis

8

Which of the following exercises consists of low-impact flexibility and muscular strength and endurance movements which emphasize proper postural alignment, core strength, and muscle balance?

A) Pilates
B) Aerobics
C) Inline skating
D) Cross-country skiing

9

Warm-up is the preparation for a physical activity by exercising or practicing gently beforehand. Each workout should begin with a warm-up. A warm-up includes 4-5 minutes of slow jogging or walking. Warming up helps avoid injury.

Which of the following about warm-up is not correct?

A) A proper warm-up should raise your body temperature by one or two degrees Celsius.
B) It is very important that you stretch before the general warm-up.
C) Jogging slowly before running is a good warm-up because it will warm the muscles and increase the heart rate.
D) Once the general warm-up has been completed, the muscles will be more elastic and it will help reduce this risk of injury.

10

Daily motions can be counted as non-locomotor skills. Picking up coins, tying shoes, and petting animals are a few of these skills.

Which of the following non-locomotor skill is developed by the movements given above?

A) Bending
B) Turning
C) Twisting
D) Stretching

11

Volleyball is a dynamic team sport that involves using the whole body to return the ball to the other side. Jumping, rolling, and kicking are commonly used to receive and return the ball to the other side.

Which of the following refers to a situation when the ball comes to rest in a player's hand?

A) Overlap

B) Held ball

C) Play over

D) Double fault

12

Summative Assessment is an overall assessment which takes place at the end of an interval, unit, key stage or year.

Which of the following about Summative assessment in PE is correct?

A) It is used to provide examination grades.

B) It is described as "Assessment of Learning" as it provides a synopsis of students' levels of attainment at the end of a specified interval.

C) Summative assessment has been asserted as the systematic recording of the pupil's overall progress and achievement, and is made up of a series of formative assessments.

D) All of the above

13

Which of the following describes the percentages of fat, bone, water and muscle in human bodies?

A) Flexibility

B) Body mass index

C) Body composition

D) Cardiovascular endurance

14

An overload is a term that refers to the excess exercise performed above the normal standard of an individual's capacity. It aims to develop the student quickly but is not always suitable for everyone.

Which of the following does not modify overload?

A) Time

B) Intensity

C) Frequency

D) Perceived exertion

73

CONTINUE ▶

## 15

Physical education was not introduced in the US until the late 1860s. Most of the youth in the country was not fit as compared to those in Europe.

Which of the following countries did not influence the development of physical education in United States?

A) Norway

B) Sweden

C) Germany

D) England

Spatial awareness refers to the ability to be aware of oneself in space, along with an understanding of the relationship of objects when there is a position change.

Which of the following refers to the sequential phases of the development of spatial awareness?

A) Locating objects relative to ones' own body in space by moving one object dependent on another object.

B) Locating objects relative to one's own body in space by positioning more than one object relative to each other and independent of the body

C) Locating one object dependent on another object by positioning the objects relative to one's own body in space.

D) Locating more than one object independent of one's body by moving the objects relative to one's own body.

17

Cardio-respiratory exercises aim to develop and enhance the body's ability to control and efficiently process the oxygen from the lungs to the bloodstream. It improves the heart's ability to pump sufficient oxygen-rich blood to the body.

Which of the following exercise principles help students on a running program improve cardio-respiratory fitness?

A) Aerobic

B) Overload

C) Specificity

D) Progression

18

Manipulative skills are the skills that use the body to manipulate an object or projectile. Being able to deflect a high-velocity object is a type of manipulative skill.

Which of the following is the proper sequential order of development for the acquisition of manipulative skills?

A) Striking, throwing, kicking, ball rolling, bouncing; volleying, trapping, catching

B) Striking, throwing, catching, trapping, kicking, ball rolling, bouncing, volleying

C) Striking, throwing, bouncing, catching, trapping, kicking, ball rolling, volleying

D) Striking, throwing, kicking, ball rolling, volleying, bouncing, catching, trapping

19

In a volleyball match, two team players have simultaneously contacted the ball above the net.

Which of the following situations refers to the simultaneous contact above the net by opponents and momentarily hold upon contact?

A) Line
B) Touch
C) Held ball
D) Double fault

20

Warm-up stretch is a preliminary exercise performed before the actual intensive exercise or training that a student may undergo. It helps loosen the muscles for easier movement in the field.

Which of the following is not recommended as a part of a warm-up exercise?

A) Using a gradual aerobic warm-up
B) Using a gradual anaerobic warm-up
C) Stretching the major muscle groups to be used in the activity
D) Using the muscles that will be utilized in the following activity

21

Flexibility can also be called as limberness. It is the range of movement in a joint or series of joint, and length in muscles that cross the joints inducing a bending motion.

Which of the following factors does not affect flexibility?

A) Age
B) Gender
C) Practice Level
D) Connective muscles

22

Which of the following sports enhances cooperation, honesty, and trust within and between teams because it relies on the players to call their own infractions and to try to play within the rules of the game?

A) Ultimate
B) Rugby
C) Football
D) Squash

23

Time extension, frequency of movement, and training intensity are indicators of performing an overload exercise. Intense training with excessive movements and low repetition count as overload exercise.

Which of the following overload principles does not apply towards improving body composition?

A) Aerobic exercise for about an hour

B) Aerobic exercise at a low intensity

C) Aerobic exercise three times per week

D) Aerobic exercise in intervals of high intensity

24

Which of the following practice alternatives would best promote motor learning and safety for potentially dangerous sports like downhill skiing and pole vaulting?

A) Part

B) Whole

C) Distributed

D) Progressive-part

25

Weightlifting is the activity of lifting heavy objects for exercise.

Which of the following weightlifting exercises should the physical education teacher suggest to an offensive lineman on the football team who wants to increase his chest power for blocking?

A) Deadlift

B) Pallof press

C) Bench press

D) Goblet squat

77

CONTINUE ▶

26

Soccer is a sport that is mainly played by using the feet to kick the ball towards the goal. Hands can only be used in certain circumstances, such as inbounding or goalkeeping.

Which of the following is the ruling to a player 'kneed' by an opponent during a ball confrontation?

A) Fair play
B) Direct free kick
C) Indirect free kick
D) Sitting it out for a period

27

Locomotor is defined as the act or power of moving from place to place. In which of the following locomotor skills, each foot have two tasks to complete before the weight is transferred to the other foot?

A) Skipping
B) Walking
C) Running
D) Galloping

28

The archery pointing system can be lax depending on the scene. An arrow that struck the target and failed to be stuck at the range can still get points accordingly.

Which of the following is the correct ruling for an arrow that struck the red target face but bounced off afterward?

A) Minus 3 points
B) Re-shoot arrow
C) 7 points awarded
D) Points will be based on the average score

29

Cardio-respiratory fitness refers to the capacity of the circulatory and respiratory systems to supply oxygen during sustained physical activity.

Which of the following exercise principle is applied when students conduct a running program to improve cardio-respiratory fitness?

A) Endurance
B) Specificity
C) Adaptability
D) Progression

CONTINUE ▶

30

Which of the following devices is worn by a walker or runner for recording the number of steps taken, thereby showing approximately the distance traveled?

A) Tanita

B) Pedometer

C) Spirometer

D) Bioelectrical impedance analyzer

31

A **tournament** is a type of contest that is participated by athletes from schools or states. An open tournament is an exception as it accepts any or all applicants that meet the requirement for competing.

Which of the following is not a type of tournament?

A) Spiral

B) Pyramid

C) Spiderweb

D) Round robin

32

Momentum is defined as the quantified measure of motion (of an object) from the product of its mass and velocity. On the other hand, **a manipulative skill**, refers to a physical motion using hands, feet, and other body parts, which can redirect or stop the momentum.

Which of the following manipulative skill uses the hands to stop the momentum of an object?

A) Rolling

B) Hitting

C) Catching

D) Trapping

33

The **Karvonen Formula** is a suggestive formula used to determine the target heart rate of an individual in his age group. The formula is not 100% accurate as it only suggests the estimated heart rate for the individual.

Which of the following is the heart rate range for 60% - 80% THR (target heart rate) for a 16 year old student with an RHR (resting heart rate) of 60?

A) 121-155 beats per minute

B) 130-170 beats per minute

C) 146-175 beats per minute

D) 149-164 beats per minute

34

Different physical activities aim to achieve different goals to be physically fit.

Which of the following physical activities is explained correctly?

A) Swimming involves every part of the body and develops its flexibility.

B) Rope jumping is a good mental exercise and it improves coordination.

C) Calisthenics develop muscle strength and agility and improves body composition, and it does not involve resistance training.

D) All of the above

80

CONTINUE ▶

35

A physical education teacher wants to have several lessons at a time. He wants students to move from one station to the next, within a specific time frame, to engage in all activities.

Which of the following teaching strategies should he use?

A) Team teaching
B) Station teaching
C) Parallel teaching
D) Cooperative teaching

36

The poor physical fitness of the American youth was discovered in the post-World War II by President Eisenhower. The recruitment of the army had required lower standards for physical fitness.

Which of the following was used to discover the poor physical conditioning of American youth?

A) Kraus-Webber Tests
B) Federal Security Agency
C) WWII Selective Service Examination
D) Organizations promoting physical fitness

37

Fat is a type of macronutrient that the body needs, along with protein and carbohydrates. It is a source of energy for the body and can be consumed while doing extraneous movements or exercise.

Which of the following are fats with room for two or more hydrogen atoms per molecule fatty acid chain?

A) Saturated
B) Unsaturated
C) Polyunsaturated
D) Monounsaturated

38

Non-locomotor skills refer to the skills that do not require moving through your feet. Using your hands and shaking them enough that it warms up is considered as a part of non-locomotor skill.

Which of the following is the proper sequential order of development for the acquisition of nonlocomotor skills?

A) Bend, stretch, sit, turn, twist, swing, sway, rock & sway, dodge, fall
B) Bend, stretch, turn, twist, swing, sit, rock & sway, shake, dodge, fall
C) Stretch, sit, bend, turn, swing, twist, shake, rock & sway, dodge, fall
D) Stretch, bend, sit, shake, turn, rock & sway, swing, twist, dodge, fall

81

CONTINUE ▶

39

Trunk extension refers to the body's capacity for full expansion and emphasizes areas such as the stomach, arms, and shoulder joints.

When students are performing trunk extension, what component of fitness does this activity assess?

A) Balance

B) Flexibility

C) Endurance

D) Subordination

40

Preventing injury comes in many different forms, such as preliminary warm-up and cooling down exercises. Maintaining a fit form also helps reduce the stress in the muscles, lessening the chances of muscle-related injuries.

Which of the following does RICE stand for in injury prevention?

A) Rest, Ice, Compression, Elevation

B) Raise, Inside, Compact, Elevation

C) Raise, Ice, Compression, Elevation

D) Rest, Inside, Compression, Elevation

41

Racquetball is a closed-door sport that requires an enclosed space so that the ball can bounce around the room.

Which of the following is the ruling if the service ball lands in front of the short line?

A) Fault

B) Reserve

C) Fair ball

D) Out-of-bounds

42

Skills development is an important part of physical education. The skills development will help the student to improve in different areas such as jumping and running.

Which of the following is defined correctly?

A) Throwing is developed through lifting heavier objects

B) Stretching is developed by reaching out to higher objects

C) Jumping is developed by jumping from a higher vantage point to a lower one

D) None of the above

43

Calisthenics forms a large variety of exercises that is performed using minimal equipment. Most of these exercises are usually performed in a metal square pole that requires the body to be above ground when you are hanging off it.

Which of the following is not developed by Calisthenics in general?

A) Power

B) Agility

C) Strength

D) Endurance

44

Athletes tend to drink more water because it helps regulate body temperature and lubricate the joints. Water also helps deliver the necessary nutrients to the body to gain energy. However, consuming too much water, or over-hydration, can dilute the sodium levels of the body.

Which of the following describes this type of condition?

A) Hypothermia

B) Hyperthermia

C) Hyponatremia

D) Hypernatremia

45

Which of the following areas of development is addressed when a teacher creates a program that develops students' appreciation and enjoyment in the group and also promotes the sense of self-worth?

A) Movement skills
B) Moral development
C) Social-emotional development
D) Communication development

46

Which of the following influenced the direction of physical education in the late 1800's the most?

A) Music
B) Religion
C) Medicine
D) Cultural sports

47

A student must warm-up at least 5-10 minutes before performing intensive exercises. It helps loosen the muscles that may be used in the exercise or game.

Which of the following is not a benefit of warming up?

A) Releasing hydrogen from myoglobin
B) Reducing the risk of musculoskeletal injuries
C) Stretching the major muscle groups to be used in the activity
D) Raising the body's core temperature in preparation for activity

48

Weight lifting is a form of exercise that helps develop or enhance the muscles on the arms, legs, and stomach. Different types of weight exercises can also target different parts of the body to develop.

When you train with weights your body's natural mechanisms automatically respond to make your muscles stronger. Which of the following refers to this situation?

A) Overload

B) Anaerobic

C) Specificity

D) Progression

49

Cardiovascular endurance is how efficiently your heart, blood vessels, and lungs supply oxygen-rich blood to working muscles during physical activity for more than 90 seconds.

Which of the following about cardiovascular endurance is not correct?

A) Cardiorespiratory endurance is also known as aerobic fitness.

B) Cardiovascular endurance can not be negatively affected by heart disease.

C) The Cooper 12 minute run test is a suitable method for measuring your cardiovascular endurance.

D) Cardiorespiratory endurance is usually measured in terms of maximum oxygen uptake

50

Weight training is a common type of strength training for developing the strength and size of skeletal muscles.

To assure safety, which of the following pieces of weight training equipment is most important?

A) Bar collars
B) Foam roller
C) Dipping Bars
D) Rubber cushions

51

An ordinary human body cannot necessarily perform above average tasks such as running as fast as a mid-speed car or lifting heavier objects like large barbells. The body's performance has something to do with the training and its extensive use.

Which of the following is the body's ability to change rapidly in direction?

A) Speed
B) Agility
C) Instinct
D) Reaction time

52

Low-calorie diets are introduced to people who would like to maintain or lose the necessary weight for their fitness. A 1200 calorie intake per day can be considered a low-calorie diet.

Which of the following is a false statement about a low-calorie diet?

A) It makes weight control easier
B) It is the way most people try to lose weight
C) Most people who "diet only" regain the weight they lose
D) It leads to excess worry about weight, food, and eating.

53

An overload exercise aims to lift the limit of the body by performing an intensive exercise, which the individual does not usually do.

Which of the following is not a part of overloading for muscle strength exercise?

A) Lifting weights every other day
B) Lifting heart rate to an intense level
C) Lifting with high resistance and low reps
D) Lifting 60% to 90% of assessed muscle strength

54

Before transferring the weight to the other foot, each foot must complete two tasks. This routine is illustrated by which of the following locomotor skills?

A) Jumping
B) Skipping
C) Side-sliding
D) Weight lifting

55

Cooperative games emphasize play rather than the competition while **team sports** are the activities in which individuals are organized into opposing teams which compete to win.

Which of the following is the contribution of the recreational group and team games such as volleyball in providing social benefits?

A) Pushing all players to their maximum capabilities to uplift the team
B) Promote enjoyment and camaraderie among participants with similar interests
C) Encourage team competition to keep winning the game
D) Keep participants of all fitness levels equally challenged

56

Social activities are introduced to students to improve their social interaction with other people through sports or games. Physical education also aims to develop a student's behavior and discipline.

Which of the following is not a social skill and value that is developed through activities?

A) Winning at all costs
B) Making judgments in groups
C) Respecting rules and property
D) Communicating and cooperating

57

The cardiovascular system transports blood throughout the body. Oxygen-rich blood is delivered in the circulation while collecting the blood with depleted oxygen levels back to the heart-lung system.

Which of the following must be done when performing activities for cardiovascular system fitness?

A) Performing it every day
B) Performing it every other day
C) Performing it for a minimum of 90 minutes
D) Performing it without developing an oxygen debt

58

A student must be able to follow instructions and perform the necessary requirements for a physical education class. Discipline must be instilled for a student to develop a behavior of being able to listen and act according to proper instruction.

Which of the following appropriate behavior in physical education is demonstrated by a teacher who modifies and develops tasks for a class?

A) Appropriate content behavior
B) Appropriate student behavior
C) Appropriate management behavior
D) Appropriate administration behavior

59

The movement of a player indicates the personal ability to manifest the acquired skills during training. The quality of movement can dictate the outcome of the skill being performed.

Which of the following quality of movement is developed by moving in a specific pattern while measuring how long it took to finish such movement?

A) Time

B) Force

C) Inertia

D) Balance

60

Static balance refers to the ability of a person to maintain the body in some fixed posture. It is also described as the ability of a person to maintain equilibrium.

Which of the following actions demonstrates static balance?

A) Maintaining a handstand position

B) Placing three limbs inside an exercise ring for 5 seconds

C) Standing in place on a balance beam

D) All of the above

61

Ms. Dianne, a physical education teacher, asks her students to keep a journal about how they felt about each activity during a physical education unit focusing on the development of health-related fitness.

What is the purpose of the activity of keeping a journal?

A) Use for differentiated instruction

B) Use for criterion-referenced grading

C) Use for standards-based instruction

D) Use for identification and recall of information

62

Transfer of learning is the dependency of human conduct, learning, or performance on prior experience.

Which of the following conditions will most likely benefit from the principle of transfer of learning when a student is learning a new complex motor skill?

A) New motor skill is similar to one already mastered.

B) New motor skill is a discrete skill rather than a continuous one.

C) The student has no previous knowledge about the new motor skill.

D) The student has the ability to openly take comments from teachers regardless of good or bad

63

Fitness plan includes exercises to help someone improve his/her health and physical condition.

Which of the following is an initial consideration in making activities for a personal fitness plan?

A) Choosing activities that are less costly and easy to execute

B) Researching other group exercise activities that can be involved

C) Determining the type of physical activities that one enjoys

D) Considering which types of activities are weather dependent and which are available year-round

64

A basketball coach separates his team in pairs. He instructs them that one will be doing chest pass and other will make a bounce pass facing each other and switch roles at the end of the line.

Which of the following would be the main objective of the activity?

A) Practicing teamwork

B) Practicing dribbling skills

C) Developing skills in passing

D) Developing offensive footwork while passing

65

Locomotor skills are the basic ways to move, the building blocks of coordination.

Which of the following locomotor skills for a five-year-old would be most difficult?

A) Jumping over low objects

B) Galloping for a bed length distance

C) Hopping on one foot from one end of a classroom to the other end

D) Climbing up and down stairs without using the handrail

66

Which of the following is not a significant component of the Whole School, Whole Community, Whole Child (WSCC) model?

A) Employee wellness

B) Health insurance for students

C) Community involvement

D) Comprehensive school health education

67

The practice session is a period of training that takes place over a set period.

Which of the following would be necessary before practice session of a folk-dance unit?

A) Repetition of the difficult steps

B) Review of the previous practice session

C) Individual presentation for future steps reference

D) Exercises and stretches to warm up muscles and joints before working on the routine

CONTINUE ▶

68

Being a natural leader and positive role model is vital in sports and physical education activities.

Which of the following is needed to be an effective natural leader and positive role model?

A) Ability to direct members on their wrongdoings

B) Ability to influence a group toward a particular goal in a nonjudgmental, collaborative way

C) Be able to intervene when a problem arises and give disciplinary measures

D) Ability to talk others into a particular course of action in an intentional way

69

Quality of movement is from the inside out. It initiates with the breath while maintaining oppositional energy and active engagement from the fingertips to the toes.

Which of the following activities would be most effective in demonstrating the quality of movement?

A) Touching bars in different heights

B) Dribbling basketball between cones

C) Throwing volleyball upwards continuously

D) Making different shapes while hanging from a bar

70

Which of the following actions should not be considered by a player when dribbling a soccer ball in a restricted space?

A) The player should stay in a slightly crouched position

B) The player should use body feints and changes of speed

C) The player should use only the dominant foot for better control

D) The player should keep the ball close to the feet

71

Muscle tone is the continuous and passive partial contraction of the muscles or the muscle's resistance to passive stretch during resting state.

Which of the following types of fitness training would you recommend for a student who wants to improve overall muscle tone and definition?

A) Single weights with decreasing number of repetitions

B) Strength training with a moderate degree of resistance and a high number of repetitions

C) Dynamic stretching involving sports movements in which reach, force, and speed are gradually increased

D) Stretching with holding exercises that muscles hold weights for a minute and gradually increasing

72

The internet is the global system of interconnected computer networks that use the Internet protocol suite (TCP/IP) to link devices worldwide.

Which of the following was the original purpose of the internet?

A) Global marketing and business transactions

B) The distribution of academic research papers

C) Sustaining the connectivity of US defense computers

D) Allowing people from all over the globe to easily share their thoughts and ideas

73

Which of the following is not considered as a use of standardized assessments?

A) To evaluate whether students have learned what they are expected to learn.
B) To determine whether educational policies are working as intended.
C) To identify gaps in student learning and academic progress.
D) To use standardized test results in curriculum evaluation.

74

The school conducted a parent/guardian meeting about the performance of physical education students.

Which of the following is the most important point of discussion?

A) Emphasizing that activities in physical education classes are all student-friendly
B) Doing surveys on the insights of the parent/guardian in their children's progress
C) Describing in detail the assessment tools and techniques used to evaluate student performance
D) Addressing student strengths and achievements in addition to areas needing improvement

75

Forward roll also called as **roly-poly** is one of the essential elements in gymnastics.

Which of the following is the most commonly encountered problem in doing the forward roll considering the primitive stage of the action?

A) Losing the curl
B) Keeping the chin tucked
C) Keeping hips and knees flexed
D) Using the hands to cushion the head contact

76

Which of the following about Observations and Inferences is not correct?

A) Observations are mere generalizations; inferences are eye-witness accounts.
B) Observations are based on information seen; inferences are based on information already known.
C) Observations may skew the truth; inferences reveal the true state regardless of speaker's claims.
D) All of these answers are correct.

A curriculum model determines the type of curriculum used; it encompasses educational philosophy, approach to teaching, and methodology.

A physical education class activity for the 5th grade student is done by the pair. One student finds out how his pair is making mistakes and students switch roles on the teacher's signal.

Which of the following is the curriculum model used by the teacher?

A) Eclectic approaches

B) Peer Teaching Model

C) Problem-solving model

D) Cooperative Learning Model

How would a wrestler learn a new takedown technique considering the applications of technology?

A) By viewing recordings of his wrestling performances

B) By reading about the proper technique and procedure on the internet

C) By viewing a series of pictures showing proper execution on a video screen

D) By exchanging e-mail messages with other wrestlers about their experience of learning the technique

Acquiring motor skills is just one part of children's development. Mastering both fine and gross motor skills are essential for children's growth and independence. Having good motor control helps children explore the world around them and also helps with their cognitive development.

Which of the following is the most challenging skill to master for children undergoing motor skill development?

A) Catching

B) Galloping

C) Throwing

D) Skipping

Stewardship is an ethic that embodies the responsible planning and management of resources.

Which of the following will develop stewardship of students toward the environment in an outdoor education program?

A) Reminding students to bring fewer things for a day out

B) Teaching students on the major viewpoints of the place

C) Requiring students to participate in environmental campaigns

D) Teaching students Leave No Trace principles and how to apply them in any outdoor setting

95   CONTINUE ▶

81

Muscle contraction is the activation of tension-generating sites within muscle fibers.

Which of the following are the means of production of force in an isometric muscle contraction?

A) As a response to extension of joint

B) As a response to a greater opposing movement with elongation

C) Through tension and muscle contraction without movement

D) Through movement generated in opposition to the downward pull of gravity

82

The most commonly known throw in disc golf is the backhand. It derives its name from tennis because the motion (having the arms cross over in front of the body, then moving outward and releasing with the arm extended before the body) is reminiscent of the tennis stroke.

Which of the following is being achieved when the back of the hand is kept parallel with the ground during a backhand disc throw, and the release is flat rather than at an angle?

A) Making the disc fly farther

B) Giving a slight backward movement after the flight

C) Forming an S-shaped pathway

D) Flying the disc diagonally to hit the ground

83

An **injury** is a damage to the body caused by an external force.

During basketball games, which of the following situations would most likely to result in an injury?

A) A distinguishable line of the court

B) Nonfunctioning overhead middle fluorescent light

C) Narrow safety zone between an end line of the court and a gym wall

D) A facilitator table located in the center of the court which is in meter-distance of the outside line

84

A kick is a physical strike using the leg: foot, heel, tibia, thigh or knee.

Which of the following would help students who fail to step forward with their kicking foot and leap onto their non-kicking foot just before the kick?

A) Set concentration on one pattern to generate controlled kick.

B) Make a mark for every step, leap, and kick off the student to monitor their kick positions.

C) Place two poly spots at the desired distances in front of each student and instruct students to step on one and leap onto the other before contacting the ball.

D) Place a plastic cone in front of each student's dominant side and instruct students to step, leap, and kick without a ball, trying to skim the cone.

85

The Internet is a global computer network providing a variety of information and communication facilities, consisting of interconnected networks using standardized communication protocols.

Which of the following is the advantage of the Internet in doing research for physical education students?

A) Finding sources of fitness equipment and materials

B) Creating a list of physical activities used throughout the world

C) Comparing the advantages and disadvantages of various physical fitness regimens

D) Locating appropriate resources for individual physical activities and nutritional needs and guidelines

CONTINUE ▶

86

Self-confidence is how you feel about your abilities and can vary from situation to situation while self-esteem reflects a person's overall subjective emotional evaluation of his or her own worth.

Which of the following type of benefit is gained from regular exercise when there is an increase in self-confidence and self-esteem through one's improvement of appearance and ability to perform tasks?

A) Physical

B) Cognitive

C) Psychological

D) Free-spirited

87

"Simon Says" is a child's game for 3 or more players where 1 player takes the role of "Simon" and issues instructions (usually physical actions such as "jump in the air" or "stick out your tongue") to the other players which should only be followed if prefaced with the phrase "Simon says".

Which of the following is the purpose of the game "Simon Says" in evaluating students' ability?

A) Develop balance and strength

B) Distinguish among locomotor skills

C) Demonstrate body awareness concepts

D) Develop teamwork and coordination skills

88

The legislation is a law which has been promulgated by a legislature or other governing body or the process of making it.

Which of the following is the leading factor in legislative and policy changes impacting physical education?

A) Increase in childhood obesity

B) Increase in cases of malnutrition

C) Increase in cases of eating disorders

D) Increase in number of students who do not engage in sports

89

Educational standards are the learning goals that students should know and be able to use at each grade level.

Which of the following will be the most probable result in a program by using national and state standards to guide the active development of a curriculum?

A) Control the number of enrolled students to maximize learning.

B) Reflect continuity and coherence across the K–12 scopes.

C) Show the level of competence in each student.

D) Assess student's knowledge before going to college.

90

A cross-curricular approach to teaching is characterized by sensitivity towards, and synthesis of, knowledge, skills, and understandings from various subject areas.

Which of the following is the benefit of cross-curricular links to physical education students?

A) Increased number of lessons learned

B) Increase in the students' time in class

C) Increase in respect of students to teachers

D) Increased awareness by students of the relevance of all subjects

91

Which of the following should a teacher initially provide in teaching a closed skill such as a free throw in basketball?

A) A varying rates of skill performance in a varying environment

B) A stable rate of skill performance in a stable environment

C) A varying rates of skill performance in a stable environment

D) A stable rate of skill performance in a varying environment

92

The adolescent growth spurt is a rapid increase in the individual's height and weight during puberty resulting from the simultaneous release of growth hormones, thyroid hormones, and androgens.

Which of the following is the result of the changes in the proportion of limb-to-torso-length when an adolescent's arms and legs grow longer?

A) Poor tissue elasticity

B) Increase in flexibility and balance

C) Formation of toned and flexible muscles

D) Periods of poor coordination and balance

93

An implement is a piece of equipment, primarily used for a particular purpose.

What is the direct relationship of the difficulty of striking a ball with a tool like a tennis racket, a bat, or golf club?

A) The difficulty of striking a ball decreases with the length of the implement.

B) The difficulty of striking a ball increases with the length of the implement.

C) The difficulty of striking a ball stays the same with the length of the implement.

D) No direct relationship on the difficulty of striking a ball with an implement.

With the help of cooperative games, students can become critical thinkers, learn to work with one another, and apply these skills to accomplish team goals.

Which of the following opportunities do cooperative games and team sports provide in developing positive traits and values for students?

A) Test individual's limit and patience.

B) Stay calm even working under pressure.

C) Study and emulate the interpersonal skills of a variety of adult role models.

D) Observe and practice character-building skills such as determination, loyalty, self control, and civility.

The forward roll is a movement in which one's body is rolled forward, by putting the head on the ground and swinging the legs over the head.

Which of the following would be the most appropriate solution of a teacher when he repeatedly observes that his students' execution of forwarding roll is unsuccessful because one student rolls in a crooked line and bumps into the next student after him?

A) Give the student separate activity to work on

B) Change the position of the student and put him into a larger area

C) Change the activity in which all can execute the act successfully

D) Observe the student's roll to assess movement technique and provide individualized instruction.

96

Spatial awareness is the ability to be aware of oneself in space. It is an organized knowledge of objects in relation to oneself in that given space. Spatial awareness also involves understanding the relationship of these objects when there is a change of position.

Which of the following activities should a teacher facilitate for his kindergarten class to learn spatial awareness?

A) Playing a tag game
B) Doing group run relay
C) Throwing ball upwards
D) Balancing on body parts

97

Field hockey is an outdoor game played on a grass field between two teams of 11 players who use long curved sticks to hit a small ball and try to score goals while indoor floor hockey is usually in the style of ice hockey, that are played on flat floor surfaces, such as a basketball court.

Which of the following would be the basic rule of field hockey and indoor floor hockey?

A) Excessive body contact or stick-to-stick contact is not allowed.
B) Players must elevate the stick above chest level when doing follow-through.
C) Players must hold the stick, on the one hand, all the time.
D) Players can hold the ball before going out of the line.

98

Self-esteem reflects a person's overall subjective emotional evaluation of his or her worth.

Which of the following does outdoor education bring to students in promoting their self-esteem?

A) Having time for meditation
B) Having alone time for self-reflection
C) Experience a sense of accomplishment in reaching a goal or destination.
D) Attempt to set personal best records each time one participates.

99

The narration is the act of telling a story, usually in some kind of chronological order. A dance teacher lets her students watch a dance performance with narration that explains the story of the dance being performed before doing their routines.

Which of the following is the benefit of narration on the students' understanding of dance?

A) Examples of giving facial expressions
B) Developing an emotional connection with other dancers
C) Showing that movement can convey meaning
D) Demonstrating artistic and aesthetic expression

School management is looking for strategies that would promote the values of their physical education programs.

Which of the following would be the most practical and effective method?

A) Create more routines that emphasize motor learning in students.

B) Give flyers with instruction to teachers and students that they also need to be sent out to the community.

C) Use a variety of media to communicate with students, families, and school community members about fitness and recreational resources, activities and their benefits.

D) Assist teachers and administrators in locating and accessing inexpensive fitness and recreational resources and facilities in the community.

CONTINUE ▶

SECTION 3 - PHYSICAL EDUCATION

#	Answer	Topic	Subtopic	#	Answer	Topic	Subtopic	#	Answer	Topic	Subtopic	#	Answer	Topic	Subtopic
1	C	TB	S4	26	B	TB	S7	51	B	TB	S2	76	B	TB	S6
2	A	TB	S4	27	A	TB	S3	52	A	TB	S2	77	B	TB	S1
3	C	TB	S6	28	C	TB	S7	53	A	TB	S2	78	A	TB	S3
4	B	TB	S4	29	B	TB	S5	54	B	TB	S1	79	D	TB	S2
5	B	TB	S7	30	B	TB	S1	55	B	TB	S2	80	D	TB	S3
6	A	TB	S4	31	A	TB	S5	56	A	TB	S4	81	C	TB	S3
7	A	TB	S7	32	C	TB	S2	57	D	TB	S2	82	A	TB	S3
8	A	TB	S3	33	C	TB	S4	58	A	TB	S1	83	C	TB	S1
9	B	TB	S4	34	D	TB	S1	59	A	TB	S2	84	C	TB	S1
10	A	TB	S2	35	B	TB	S1	60	D	TB	S3	85	D	TB	S1
11	B	TB	S2	36	A	TB	S7	61	A	TB	S1	86	C	TB	S2
12	D	TB	S5	37	C	TB	S4	62	A	TB	S2	87	C	TB	S2
13	C	TB	S3	38	D	TB	S4	63	C	TB	S1	88	A	TB	S3
14	D	TB	S2	39	B	TB	S4	64	C	TB	S2	89	B	TB	S1
15	A	TB	S6	40	A	TB	S7	65	C	TB	S2	90	D	TB	S1
16	B	TB	S6	41	A	TB	S3	66	B	TB	S3	91	B	TB	S1
17	C	TB	S4	42	D	TB	S2	67	D	TB	S3	92	D	TB	S3
18	D	TB	S4	43	A	TB	S2	68	B	TB	S1	93	B	TB	S3
19	C	TB	S3	44	C	TB	S4	69	D	TB	S3	94	D	TB	S2
20	B	TB	S2	45	C	TB	S2	70	C	TB	S3	95	D	TB	S3
21	D	TB	S4	46	C	TB	S3	71	B	TB	S2	96	D	TB	S2
22	A	TB	S2	47	A	TB	S2	72	C	TB	S6	97	A	TB	S3
23	C	TB	S2	48	C	TB	S4	73	D	TB	S5	98	C	TB	S2
24	D	TB	S2	49	B	TB	S4	74	D	TB	S2	99	C	TB	S1
25	C	TB	S2	50	A	TB	S3	75	A	TB	S3	100	C	TB	S1

Topics & Subtopics

Code	Description	Code	Description
SB1	Planning Instruction	SB5	Student Assessment
SB2	Student Growth & Development	SB6	Communication, Collaboration & Technology
SB3	Planning Activities	SB7	Management & Motivation
SB4	Health-Related Physical Fitness	TB	Physical Education

CONTINUE ▶

TEST DIRECTION

DIRECTIONS

Read the questions carefully and then choose the ONE best answer to each question.

Be sure to allocate your time carefully so you are able to complete the entire test within the testing session. You may go back and review your answers at any time.

You may use any available space in your test booklet for scratch work.

Questions in this booklet are not actual test questions but they are the samples for commonly asked questions.

This test aims to cover all topics which may appear on the actual test. However some topics may not be covered.

Studying this booklet will be preparing you for the actual test. It will not guarantee improving your test score but it will help you pass your exam on the first attempt.

Some useful tips for answering multiple choice questions;

- Start with the questions that you can easily answer.

- Underline the keywords in the question.

- Be sure to read all the choices given.

- Watch for keywords such as NOT, always, only, all, never, completely.

- Do not forget to answer every question.

CONTINUE ▶

1

Clique refers to a circle or group of people sharing common interests, views or features and spending time together.

Which of the following best describes why adolescents join clique?

A) Create larger connections.

B) Gain high respect above others.

C) Expose themselves to a different environment.

D) Satisfy the need to have an alternative identity.

2

Addiction is repeatedly engaging with drugs, alcohol, or gambling despite the harm it can cause since it has become a habit and source of pleasure. However, addicted users in a family can cause fear and hardship to the whole family.

Which of the following can be the most useful action in dealing with a family member's addiction to improve the family's wellness?

A) Temporarily prioritize the addicted family needs over other family matters.

B) Do everything not to have contact with the addicted family member since he can be harmful anytime.

C) Think of ways to adapt to the situation and let the addicted family member do his addiction until he regrets it.

D) Confront the addicted family member about it since it will be a problem not only for him but through the family and seek professional help for him.

3

Mira is participating in a conflict resolution or peer mediation program.

Which of the following would Mira most likely learn first from attending the program in terms of managing anger?

A) How to say "No" and be firm
B) How to listen carefully with respect
C) How to express "I" statements effectively
D) How to think of different solutions and possibilities

4

If one day a parent becomes seriously ill, their children will be the most affected.

Which of the following will help children to cope with this type of situation effectively?

A) Research on medical treatments to understand them.
B) Give opportunities where feelings can be shown completely.
C) Relieve stress by spending more time with extended family.
D) Attend psychotherapy every week to help in managing any changes in behavior.

5

A **gender role** refers to the accepted and appropriate behaviors that are culturally defined such as masculinity and femininity.

Which of the following typically exerts the most significant influence on the development of gender roles?

A) Competency
B) Socialization process
C) Judgments to people
D) Maslow's hierarchy of needs

CONTINUE ▶

6

Maria and Kevin are childhood friends. However, all relationships undergo trials and misunderstanding. Maria poked up Kevin's low grades in class and this caused them to become estranged. Maria feels sorry but doesn't know how to start a conversation since Kevin always ignores her.

Which of the following could be the most useful communication method for them to help refresh their relationship?

A) Undergoing counseling

B) Assuming the situation didn't happen.

C) Accepting responsibility about the situation

D) Telling both sides excuses on how the situation happened.

7

In a situation wherein a child asks for her parents' advice on a certain matter about her school, which of the following best promotes a good and healthy relationship between the child and the parent?

A) Showing support on the child's decision.

B) Discussing the matter but making the final decision for the child.

C) Telling the child to ask for advice from the school teacher instead.

D) Telling the child to ask for advice from the school guidance counselor instead.

8

Which of the following is the domain of learning about sports rules, traditions, and history?

A) Interactions

B) Mental skills under cognitive

C) Emotional skills under affective

D) Physical skills under psychomotor

9

A **strain** is a stretching or tearing of muscle or tendon.

Which of the following will most likely to result in a muscle pull or strain?

A) Doing varying exercises every session

B) Interchanging work of upper and lower body every other day

C) Using static stretching rather than dynamic stretching to cool down after strength training

D) Exercising a particular muscle group without working for its opposing muscle group (e.g., quadriceps but not hamstrings)

10

Intercultural communication refers to communication between people from different cultures or social groups verbally and nonverbally.

Which of the following would best describe the effect of intercultural communication?

A) Communication and courtesy gestures are the same in all cultures.

B) Cultural groups close to each other have fewest communication problems.

C) Communication desire must be higher on the majority culture comprising the group.

D) Nonverbal expressions and behaviors may be interpreted in different ways by people of different cultures.

11

Which of the following instruments can be used to determine an individual's body fat composition most effectively?

A) A skinfold caliper

B) Scales and a height-weight chart

C) Hydrostatic body composition analysis

D) Measurements of the circumference of the waist, hips, thighs, and arms of the person.

12

Information about public health is readily accessible for communal use. However, it can be occasionally confusing when deciding on what health products and services to utilize and which health behaviors to practice and execute.

Which of the following options is essential for people to make the most suitable judgments about their health?

A) Acquire health insurance.

B) Request for recommendations.

C) Be knowledgeable about health.

D) Search and study health in internet websites.

Being a college student, you are trained to prepare the life of being professional and being away from home. David, a freshman student, was dropped off on his dormitory by his dad. Being away for the first time, David said "goodbye" with a heavy heart to his father, but they both agreed to have electronic communication from time to time to update each other.

Which of the following best describes the benefit and value of this mediated communication?

A) Maximizing the use of technology

B) Always having support in all areas especially finances

C) Maintaining an existing relationship during a transition period

D) Scheduling frequent visitations to help in school requirements

Peer mediation is the process of setting two or more students involved in a conflict meet in a confidential setting to solve their problems with the help of a trained student mediator.

Which of the following must students need to learn first in the peer mediation program or to manage their anger in conflict situations?

A) Strong rejection response

B) Listening with care and respect

C) Exploring creative alternatives

D) Finding someone to let out all the anger piled inside

Which of the following is the best range of maximum heart rate, in terms of percentage, in characterizing a student's exercise for health related fitness in physical education class?

A) 20-40%

B) 40-60%

C) 60-85%

D) 85-100%

Adolescence refers to the transition period between childhood and adulthood that involves big changes in physical, intellectual, personal and social development. It has been considered as a crucial stage in developing adaptable and logical thinking since this stage is where teens are faced with many issues and decisions.

Which of the following effects will most likely develop on an adolescent's social development from a positive peer pressure through membership in a clique?

A) Comparing life challenges

B) Increasing communication skills

C) Creating a wide social network

D) Promoting feelings of competency

17

A person who is capable of understanding and applying acquired health information to personal health choices and behaviors has a better chance of managing a chronic disease.

Which of the following consequences has been the most closely related to inadequate health literacy among people diagnosed with Type 2 diabetes?

A) Dealing with diabetes successfully

B) Struggling to maintain glycemic control

C) Engaging in diabetes learning programs

D) Low percentage of diabetes-related dilemmas

18

The potential of a young man to become a perpetrator of violence is increased by which of the following risk factors?

A) Low connections with friends in the school

B) Being exposed to media that shows violence

C) Peer pressure that results in a negative feeling

D) Joining a social clique

19

Upon opening her social media account, Risa, a high school student, receives a message from an anonymous sender containing lewd messages.

Which of the following did Risa experience?

A) Harassment: Unwelcome conduct that is based on race, religion, sex, and etc

B) Defamation: The action of damaging a third party's good reputation

C) Abuse: Treating someone with cruelty, especially regularly and repeatedly.

D) Teasing: Making fun of someone in a playful way

20

Physical health is critical for overall well-being and is the most visible of the various dimensions of health, which also include social, intellectual, emotional, spiritual and environmental health.

Most personal traits are interdependent and changes in one may affect another. Which of the following personal traits is affected by your physical health?

A) Gender

B) Ethnic heritage

C) Self-confidence

D) Cultural background

Kinesthesis is the ability of the person to feel movements of the limbs and body.

Which of the following is the other name for kinesthesis?

A) Reflex action
B) Coordination
C) Proprioception
D) Tonic neck response

Severe illness is where a person has detrimental defects that affect his or her daily function, needs high case treatments due to complicated symptoms and has a high chance of mortality.

Which of the following will not help a child adjust to the situation wherein a parent falls seriously ill?

A) Provide opportunities to express feelings unconditionally.
B) Allow the child not to go to school and do leisure activities.
C) Allow extended family to be with the child to help her with her daily needs.
D) Schedule a meeting with a therapist to handle emotional and behavioral changes.

23

Prosocial behavior refers to the voluntary behavior in helping others such as donating, sharing, giving gifts and obeying the rules.

Which of the following development closely links the growth of prosocial behavior toward peers in young children with ages between 5 and 8?

A) Choosing people to deal with

B) Having empathy for other people

C) Opting to use nonverbal communication frequently

D) Explaining the long-term benefits and costs of interpersonal relationships

24

Which of the following do you call a group of close relatives that live together or close to each other?

A) Foster family

B) Nuclear family

C) Blended family

D) Extended family

25

Addiction to drugs, alcohol, or gambling, affects not only the individual experiencing it but also the people surrounding him.

Which of the following can improve family wellness by dealing with a family member's addiction most effectively?

A) Confront the addicted family member and ask for professional help.

B) Any problems caused by addiction may be ignored by the family members.

C) Prioritize the addicted family member by focusing and giving all the attention he or she needs.

D) Try to avoid the family member that is suffering from addiction not to experience any difficulties caused by them.

26

Every weekend, Paul visits his parent's home together with his siblings for a weekly communication meeting where they discuss the issues or problems that they have and receive support from each other.

Which of the following is the benefit of this practice for each family member?

A) The family member's ability to have their sense of fulfillment.

B) The family member's ability to prevent any negative behaviors.

C) The family member's ability to manage flexible patterns of behavior.

D) The family member's ability to improve their problem-solving skills effectively.

27

Which of the following do messages of a speaker that begin with "I" emphasize?

A) A person is assigned for commenting.
B) Judging a person for something he or she made.
C) The emotions that resulted for the speaker are emphasized.
D) Making a person feel down for what he or she said.

28

Dino and Maria, a newlywed young couple, recently had a baby daughter named Ella who is six months old today.

As a young parent, which of the following skills must they learn to make appropriate parenting decisions?

A) Social
B) Career
C) Management
D) Communication

29

Wendy discovered that Christian, her ten-year-old son, stole candy from the grocery store.

To deal with this incident, which of the following behavior management practices should Wendy use?

A) Do not give the child allowance as a payment for the stolen item.
B) Ban the child from doing his favorite activities for an indefinite period.
C) Make the child write "Stealing is wrong" in a bond paper, back-to-back.
D) Return to the store and pay for the item stolen to teach the child that stealing is not right.

30

Greg and Megan are just started dating, and they are discussing each other's responsibilities in the relationship.

Which of the following is an important responsibility of both of them?

A) Assessing one another based on how he or she is viewed by others.

B) Always tabulating the good and bad sides of staying in a relationship.

C) Making a discussion about how they could support each other's long-term life plans.

D) Keeping their lines of communication open especially regarding issues and concerns about their relationship.

31

An **infant** is the stage of a human from birth to one-year-old where she needs much attention and care since she cannot do things on herselves yet.

Which of the following developments is greatly influenced by the ability of an infant to form healthy, secure attachments to caregivers?

A) Social skills

B) Independence

C) Decision making

D) Language acquisition

Dating violence refers to abusive behavior such as physical, sexual threats or emotional aggression towards a romantic relationship.

Which of the following strategies can a health education program best help students in preventing teen dating violence?

A) Explain what type of behavior is considered as abusive.

B) Let dating students learn forgiveness when one has committed abusive behavior.

C) Help students, their families, and school staff discuss behaviors, social and cultural influences that can foster violence.

D) Create harsh punishments such as expulsion to students who will commit threats, unwanted physical contact, and harassment.

On May 2016, a fire accident caused hundreds of families the loss of their homes, businesses, and investments. The incident had put their state on calamity where any donation would matter, and also psychological help was sought to help the families to cope with the tragedy.

Which of the following would be an effective strategy to help families overcome the situation and refresh their lives?

A) Wait on donations to arrive.

B) Collaborate on dealing with the immediate situation.

C) Determine the culprit who started the fire and let him or her pay for what he or she has done.

D) Transfer to nearby areas and ask them if they could let the families in until they could rebuild their homes.

34

In a parents' meeting, Dina, a mother of three, shares about how open they are as a family. Each week, they decide a specific day, time and place where they can meet and talk about their whole week activities. Each of the family members has the chance to express his or her thoughts and even bothering thoughts entirely. In turn, family members will carefully listen and express their feelings and opinions.

Which of the following is the benefit of these meetings for each family member?

A) Overcoming challenges together.

B) Setting and achieving shared goals.

C) Developing effective problem solving skills.

D) All of the above

35

Kai and Jennie are newlyweds. They decided to build their house in the city considering the proximity of their location to their work address. Jennie is an only child, and her father died a few years ago leaving her mother alone in their ancestral house. Kai and Jennie asked her mother to live with them to lessen her sadness, and she accepts it too.

Which of the following types of diverse family structures is about to be created?

A) Adoptive

B) Extended

C) Polyamorous

D) Nontraditional

36

Which of the following websites provides practical information to individuals, health professionals, nutrition educators, and the food industry to help consumers build healthier diets with resources and tools for dietary assessment, nutrition education, and other user-friendly nutrition information?

A) Calorie Lab

B) Nourished Kitchen

C) USDA ChooseMyPlate

D) Consumer Reports: Health

37

Iris belongs to a family of five with her siblings' ages ranging from 12 to 18. Five years ago, Iris' family lost their family home in a fire.

However, her family learned to cope with the changes caused by this crisis with the help of which of the following strategies?

A) Depending on others' support.

B) Working with each other to deal with the situation at hand.

C) Identifying the cause of the crisis that brought them the problem.

D) Designating one of the family members to be responsible for the decision-making.

CONTINUE ▶

38

The direct measurement of the rate of oxygen consumption during exercise is primarily determined by which of the following parameter?

A) VO2 max

B) Pulse rate

C) Minute ventilation

D) Red blood cell count

39

Which of the following is the best choice of available fitness tests for a teacher to use to assess students with disabilities?

A) Fitnessgram

B) Basic Fitness test

C) Limited fitness activity

D) Brockport Physical Fitness Test

40

Nonverbal communication refers to communication that doesn't involve speaking. It can be through facial expressions, body language or facial expression.

Which of the following are the benefits of nonverbal communication?

A) It improves verbal communication.

B) It can help a person to relate, engage, and establish meaningful interactions in everyday life.

C) Posture, vocal tone and eye contact can deliver subtle messages that can convey trustworthiness.

D) All of the above

41

Total daily calorie needs are the number of calories per day that is needed to maintain daily activities.

Which of the following stages of growth and development needs the highest amount of total daily calorie?

A) Infancy

B) Adolescence

C) Early adulthood

D) Late adulthood

Four persons' daily calorie intake and daily calorie expenditure are given below;

• Roy's daily intake is 3,000 calories and his daily expenditure is also 3,000 calories.

• Jane has 3,000 daily intakes of calories while she has a daily expenditure of 2,000 calories.

• Caleb has a daily intake of 2,000 and a daily expenditure of 2,800 calories.

• Arianna has a daily intake of 1,000 and a daily expenditure of 4,000 calories.

Who among the four persons would most likely to lose weight safely?

A) Roy

B) Jane

C) Caleb

D) Arianna

Cooling down is an easy exercise, done after a more intense activity, to allow the body to gradually transition to a resting or near-resting state while stretching is a form of physical exercise in which a specific muscle or tendon is deliberately flexed.

Which of the following is the benefit of doing cool-down and stretching activities after strenuous cardiorespiratory fitness activities?

A) Prevent an abrupt decrease in the glucose level

B) Prevent the reduction of carbohydrates and fat composition in the body

C) Prevent muscle soreness and blood pooling in the extremities

D) Trigger a final surge in metabolic rate before the body reverts to a resting state

CONTINUE ▶

44

A mother wants to determine what her 10-year-old child needs for bone growth and development.

Which of the following nutritional areas should be focused?

A) Adequate fiber intake
B) Adequate calcium intake
C) Adequate vitamin B intake
D) Adequate potassium intake

45

Aerobic exercises are any of various sustained exercises such as jogging, rowing, swimming, or cycling that stimulate and strengthen the heart and lungs.

By doing regular aerobic exercises, which of the following is the best physiological adaptation in the body?

A) The maximum heartbeat increases
B) The heart can pump more blood throughout the body
C) The lungs are being filtered out of toxins to improve breathing
D) The body is better able to produce energy from fat stored as triglycerides

46

Which of the following about the Society of Health and Physical Educators (SHAPE AMERICA) is not correct?

A) Its mission is to enhance knowledge, improve professional practice, and increase support for high-quality physical education.
B) It provides programs and resources to support health and physical educators at every level.
C) American Alliance for Health and Recreation and Dance (AAHPERD) were previously given names of it.
D) It has been founded in 1985 and it is a membership organization of health and physical education professionals.

47

The most common problem encountered in most characteristic of the primitive stage of forward rolling is due to which of the following problems?

A) The curl is lost
B) The chin is tucked
C) Head contact by hands
D) The knees and hips are flexed

CONTINUE ▶

48

Diabetes is a group of metabolic disorders in which there are high blood sugar levels over a prolonged period.

Which of the following is the benefit of exercise on treatment plans of diabetic people?

A) Reduce the build-up of glucose in the blood

B) Prevent diabetes-induced changes in vision

C) Increase the production of insulin in the pancreas

D) Reduce body weight of diabetic people

49

In order for a physical education teacher to establish good classroom management, which of the following would be the best to do at the beginning of the school year?

A) Teaching the basics of an activity

B) Making posters for announcements

C) Letting the students do fitness tests whenever they want

D) Having an organized system of rules, records, lesson with the participation of students

50

A risk factor is something that increases your chance of getting a disease.

Which of the following modifiable risk factors are associated with coronary artery disease according to the American Heart Association?

A) Age and family history

B) Age and ethnic background

C) Stress and physical inactivity

D) Smoking and alcohol consumption

51

Which of the following are the two principles of modern muscle strength and endurance conditioning followed by a person who lifted a newborn calf onto his shoulders each day until the calf became fully mature?

A) Retention and stress

B) Progression and intensity

C) Overload and progression

D) Strength and variable resistance

52

Which of the following improvements is experienced by people who do yoga according to the Mayo Clinic?

A) Faster thinking, increase in appetite, and clearer eyesight

B) Healthier skin, digestive health, and becoming more active

C) Production of testosterone, clearer eyesight, and younger looks

D) Becoming more fit, better management of chronic conditions, and reduced stress

53

Carbohydrate is any of a large group of organic compounds occurring in foods and living tissues and including sugars, starch, and cellulose.

Which of the following are the two main functions of carbohydrates in the body?

A) Building and repairing body tissues

B) Providing energy for cells and maintaining an energy reserve

C) Synthesizing and secreting complex fatty acid substances

D) Repairing damaged cells and creating new ones

54

Which of the following best describes the effect of increasing rates of sedentary activity and poor dietary practices over rates of physical activities in adolescents?

A) Increase in stress related disease

B) Increase in fatigue related diseases

C) Increase in mineral deficiency diseases

D) Increase in incidence of obesity related diseases

55

Amphetamine is a central nervous stimulant which speeds up the messages travelling between the brain and the body.

Which of the following illustrates a primary short term effect of amphetamines on the sports performance of the athletes?

A) The risk of injury decreases
B) Feelings of alertness increases
C) Thinking process decreases
D) The growth of muscles increases

56

The study shows strong and consistent evidence from observational studies that physical inactivity and poor fitness are associated with higher illness and death from all causes.

Which of the following diseases occurs mostly in people with poor fitness level and inactivity to physical activities?

A) Migraines
B) Bacterial infection
C) Fever and allergies
D) High blood pressure

57

In order to learn a new takedown technique, which of the following technology applications would best support a wrestler?

A) Gathering information from co-wrestlers
B) Proper execution of viewed pictures on a video screen
C) Reading about the proper technique and procedure on the internet
D) Watching other wrestler's performance

58

In order to assess the skills of students during a basketball skills unit, which of the following would be the most appropriate way for a physical education?

A) Having them watch basketball games

B) Having them make an essay about basketball

C) Matching two teams and watching which team will win

D) When moving through the unit, assessing learners by developing a rubric

59

Why does the warm-up period before exercise help in preserving the joints?

A) Because it encourages the uptake of lactic acid.

B) Because it activates the sympathetic nervous system.

C) Because it increases the proportion of blood in the thoracic cavity.

D) Becuase it stimulates the release of synovial fluid which lubricates the joints.

60

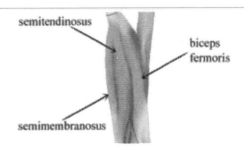

The hamstring muscle group consists of three separate muscles; the semitendinosus, semimembranosus and biceps femoris. They originate from the lower part of the pelvis and insert into the back of the shin bone. When contracting they mainly bend the knee and extend the hip joint.

One of your students has been strained in his hamstring muscle. Which of the following pieces would be the proper treatment?

A) Applying ice and compressing the leg

B) Applying ice and stretching the leg

C) Applying heat and compressing the leg

D) Applying heat and stretching the leg

61

Tendon Structure

Tendon is a flexible but inelastic cord of strong fibrous collagen tissue.

Which of the following is the main function of tendons in the skeletal system?

A) Attach bones to muscles

B) Attach bones to other bones

C) Attach ligaments to muscle fibers

D) Act as the source of calcium phosphate

62

Which of the following should be emphasized to children to have healthy eating practices and patterns?

A) Stimulate growth hormone production faster

B) Increase endurance and stamina without exercise

C) Reduce time for sleep to have more play time

D) Help prevent both short and longterm health problems such as colds, dental cavities, and obesity

Standing toe touch is bending at the waist, keeping your legs straight until you can relax and let your upper body hang down in front of you. Let your arms and hands hang down naturally.

Which of the following is the main reason that a straight-legged standing toe-touch is a high-risk exercise?

A) Maximizes hamstring stretch reflex

B) Elongates cervical ligaments causing muscle sore

C) Increases pressure on lumbar disks and overstretch lumbar ligaments

D) Uses the latissimus dorsi as a shoulder extensor, which hyper-extends the shoulders.

The fitness program is a plan to help someone improve their health and physical condition.

Which of the following sets of health-related components is emphasized in a personal fitness program that performs appropriate stretching exercises during warmup and cool down for both jogging, 3 days a week for 30–45 minutes, and weight lifting, 3 days a week?

A) Cardiorespiratory endurance, muscular strength, and flexibility

B) Cardiorespiratory endurance, body composition, and flexibility

C) Cardiorespiratory endurance, muscular strength, and agility

D) Cardiorespiratory endurance, agility, and flexibility

65

After every vigorous physical activity, cooling down is performed.

Which of the following is not an immediate physiological benefit of cooldown?

A) Cooldown reduces the risk of cardiac irregularities

B) Cooldown prevents blood from pooling in the legs

C) Cooldown promotes the reduction of cholesterol in the blood

D) Cooldown increases the rate of lactic acid removal from the blood and skeletal muscle

66

Nutrition is the process of providing or obtaining the food necessary for health and growth.

To promote optimum growth and development in young children, which of the following is the suggested nutritional practice?

A) Consuming high dietary fiber for good digestion

B) Consuming more protein to aid in developing more muscles

C) Consuming more fatty foods to increase stored energy

D) Consuming three moderately large meals and avoiding or limiting snacks and treats to promote desirable eating patterns

67

Which of the following shows linear relationship between the physiological factor and oxygen consumption?

A) Work rate, heart rate, cardiac rate

B) Blood pressure, work rate, minute ventilation

C) Red blood cell count, blood type, respiration rate

D) Pulse rate, red blood cell count, core temperature

68

Cross-training refers to combining exercises of other disciplines, different than that of the athlete in training. Swimming and jogging could be an example of cross-training activities.

Which of the following is the best physiological change in the body after weeks of doing cross-training activities?

A) Increased weight of muscles

B) Improved bone mass and strength

C) Improved ratio of high-density lipoproteins (HDLs) to low-density lipoproteins (LDLs)

D) Increased length of long bones and decreased length of tendons attached to long bones

69

Body composition is used to describe the percentages of fat, bone, water, and muscle in bodies.

Which of the following is the main concern of body composition as a component of health-related fitness?

A) Muscle formation in the body

B) Maintenance of bone mass in the body

C) Relative proportions of fat and lean tissue in the body

D) The relative amount of vitamins present in the body

70

In physical education class, the maximum heart rate that should characterize students' exercise for health-related fitness is best expressed by which of the following heart rate percentage?

A) A maximum heart rate of 10-35%

B) A maximum heart rate of 35-60%

C) A maximum heart rate of 60-85%

D) A maximum heart rate of 85-95%

71

Negligence is a term that means carelessness or a breach of an obligation.

In case of a student acquiring injury in a physical education class, which of the following teaching practices will protect the teacher from possible charges of negligence?

A) Doing more group feedback discussions than individual evaluation

B) Allowing students not to participate in activities they are not fine doing

C) Ensuring that the students always have a written copy of instructions

D) Providing students with appropriate instruction based on recommended skills progressions

Cardiopulmonary resuscitation (CPR) is a lifesaving technique useful in many emergencies, including heart attack or near drowning.

Which of the following is the main purpose of rescue breathing and chest compressions in doing CPR?

A) Produce electric shock to retrieve heart rhythm

B) Remove any object trapped inside the heart

C) Provide artificial ventilation for a victim who is in severe respiratory distress

D) Oxygenate and circulate the blood in a victim whose heart has stopped beating

SECTION 4 - HEALTH EDUCATION

#	Answer	Topic	Subtopic	#	Answer	Topic	Subtopic	#	Answer	Topic	Subtopic	#	Answer	Topic	Subtopic
1	D	TA	S3	19	A	TA	S3	37	B	TA	S3	55	B	TA	S1
2	D	TA	S3	20	C	TA	S1	38	A	TA	S1	56	D	TA	S1
3	B	TA	S3	21	C	TA	S1	39	D	TA	S2	57	B	TA	S2
4	B	TA	S3	22	B	TA	S3	40	D	TA	S3	58	D	TA	S2
5	B	TA	S3	23	B	TA	S3	41	B	TA	S2	59	D	TA	S1
6	C	TA	S3	24	D	TA	S3	42	C	TA	S2	60	A	TA	S2
7	A	TA	S3	25	A	TA	S3	43	C	TA	S2	61	A	TA	S1
8	B	TA	S1	26	D	TA	S3	44	B	TA	S1	62	D	TA	S2
9	D	TA	S1	27	C	TA	S3	45	D	TA	S1	63	C	TA	S2
10	D	TA	S3	28	D	TA	S3	46	D	TA	S2	64	A	TA	S2
11	C	TA	S2	29	D	TA	S3	47	A	TA	S1	65	C	TA	S1
12	C	TA	S1	30	D	TA	S3	48	A	TA	S2	66	D	TA	S2
13	C	TA	S3	31	A	TA	S3	49	D	TA	S2	67	D	TA	S1
14	B	TA	S3	32	C	TA	S3	50	C	TA	S2	68	C	TA	S1
15	C	TA	S1	33	B	TA	S3	51	C	TA	S1	69	C	TA	S1
16	D	TA	S3	34	D	TA	S3	52	D	TA	S1	70	C	TA	S2
17	B	TA	S1	35	B	TA	S3	53	B	TA	S1	71	D	TA	S2
18	A	TA	S3	36	C	TA	S2	54	D	TA	S1	72	D	TA	S1

Topics & Subtopics

Code	Description	Code	Description
SA1	Health Knowledge	SA3	Healthy Interpersonal Relationships
SA2	Health Instruction	TA	Health Education

CONTINUE ▶

TEST DIRECTION

DIRECTIONS

Read the questions carefully and then choose the ONE best answer to each question.

Be sure to allocate your time carefully so you are able to complete the entire test within the testing session. You may go back and review your answers at any time.

You may use any available space in your test booklet for scratch work.

Questions in this booklet are not actual test questions but they are the samples for commonly asked questions.

This test aims to cover all topics which may appear on the actual test. However some topics may not be covered.

Studying this booklet will be preparing you for the actual test. It will not guarantee improving your test score but it will help you pass your exam on the first attempt.

Some useful tips for answering multiple choice questions;

- Start with the questions that you can easily answer.

- Underline the keywords in the question.

- Be sure to read all the choices given.

- Watch for keywords such as NOT, always, only, all, never, completely.

- Do not forget to answer every question.

1

Many different sports have similarities in training, such as softball and baseball. Volleyball and basketball can also be similar in endurance training.

Which of the following technique is used to facilitate the cognitive learning by using a similar movement skill from the previous lesson to the new one?

A) Longer instruction

B) Conceptual thinking

C) Innovative learning

D) Transfer of learning

2

The human body utilizes fat as an energy source since it is the primary storage of energy in the body. The body requires a sufficient amount of fat for good health; however, consuming too much fat may be unhealthy.

Among the methods listed, which of the following can most accurately determine a person's body fat content?

A) Skin-fold calipers

B) Scales and a height-weight chart

C) Underwater weighing or hydrostatic weighing

D) Calculating the circumference of hips, waist, thighs, and arms

CONTINUE ▶

3

A physical education instructor anticipates and prevents a potential injury, watches for some hidden injuries, and takes an evaluation for injury history for the whole class.

Which of the following injury prevention strategy is demonstrated with this?

A) Participant screening

B) Proper use of equipment

C) Maintaining hiring standards

D) Proper procedures for emergencies

4

If a machine can outperform the body, then the body can also outperform the machine in its adaptability. The mechanical principles can be applied to the body, unlike the other way around.

Which of the following movement concept describes the application of the mechanical principles of balance, time, and force?

A) Body Awareness

B) Effort Awareness

C) Spatial Awareness

D) Mental Awareness

A rural school seeks to increase its access to technological resources for teaching and learning. However, the school is significantly experiencing funding problems.

Which action should the school administrators do to achieve this goal?

A) Collaborate with educators from the more affluent and technologically advanced schools to learn various strategies.

B) Seek support from local businesses that may have interest in having partnerships in achieving the school's goal.

C) Cut other areas of the school's budget plan and use it to increase the technology funding.

D) Solicit for public assistance in raising funds for the school through publicizing its needs in newspapers and other local media.

Systematic Observational Evaluation is the type of assessment that is used to evaluate a student through systematic observation. The student's performance can be previewed by using the recorded skills and evaluated accordingly.

Which of the following is a Systematic Observational Evaluation?

A) Iowa recording
B) Snap recording
C) Vital recording
D) Duration recording

7

A student is medically certified as paraplegic and still goes to school. Although this is the case, he still wants to attend his physical education classes in his capacity.

Which of the following federal legislative act entitles his right to do so?

A) Title IX
B) Title XIII
C) PL 94-142
D) PE 94-142

8

Locomotor skills are the basics of coordination for the body. It is the skills of moving such as walking and running.

Which of the following locomotor skills uses one foot to take off and land onto a surface?

A) Jumping
B) Hopping
C) Leaping
D) Vaulting

9

When a volleyball player receives the ball with an appropriate reception but bounces on her shoulder thereafter, which of the following ruling is applied?

A) Score
B) Foul
C) Legal hit
D) Two-touch count

10

Which of the following concept is promoted by throwing a ball back and forth against your partner with increasing distance?

A) Range
B) Speed
C) Precision
D) Accuracy

11

Aerobic exercises intend to expose the body to exercises that promote healthy breathing and blood circulation. The body movements must result in a higher heart rate and lung capacity.

Which of the following is improved by an aerobic dance?

A) Balance

B) Flexibility

C) Body coordination

D) Bodily muscle improvement

12

The history of physical education dates back to ancient Ancient Greek. The philosophy behind physical education teaches students the mechanics and importance of the physical activity.

Which of the following about history and philosophy of physical education is incorrect?

A) Eclectics refers to the modern physical education philosophy that combines beliefs from different philosophies.

B) Pragmatism refers to as the first lesson on physical education based on perception.

C) Friedrich Jahn is the father of modern physical education classes.

D) None of the above

13

Body awareness refers to a person's understanding of his or her body parts and their capability of movement.

Which of the following statements about movement and awareness is not correct?

A) Effort Awareness refers to the ability to develop a conscious recognition of one's body movements while doing various physical activities.

B) Spatial Awareness involves students making decisions about an object's positional changes in space.

C) Time management of movement is developed when freely letting students do various activities no matter how long it takes until the task is done.

D) None of the above

14

People are obsessed with losing weight. Health experts reveal that a person must burn 3,500 calories to lose one pound.

Physical Activity	Calories Burned per Hour
Aerobics	500
Bicycling	590
Dancing	330
Walking	460

Which of the following activities can make an individual lose exactly one pound (Refer to the information given above)?

A) Half an hour of bicycling every day for one week

B) An hour of dancing every day for one week

C) Half an hour of walking every day for one week

D) An hour of aerobics every day for one week

15

Bowling refers to a series of sports or leisure activities in which a player rolls or throws a bowling ball towards a target.

Which of the following basic bowling skills should be reviewed first before practicing?

A) Proper stance

B) Tallying scores

C) Retrieving the bowling ball

D) Choosing a grip that is comfortable

16

Due to the size of the court, tennis players tend to strengthen their shots from time to time and catch their opponents off guard. Buying as much time possible can let a player play his tactics better.

Which of the following shots would be appropriate if a player intends to buy time to return to the court?

A) Lob shot

B) Dink shot

C) Long shot

D) Overhead shot

17

One way to measure the body's readiness for exercise is to use the **body mass index (BMI)** measurement. BMI is a person's weight in kilograms (kg) divided by his or her height in meters squared. It can be used to screen for weight categories that may lead to health problems but it is not diagnostic of the body fatness or health of an individual.

Which one of the following is the BMI score that indicates obesity?

A) 14
B) 22
C) 26
D) 31

18

Legislature refers to a deliberative assembly with authority to make laws for a political unit.

Which of the following professional organizations works with legislatures?

A) Amateur Athletic Union (AAU)
B) American College of Sports Medicine (ACSM)
C) National Collegiate Athletic Association (NCAA)
D) American Alliance for Health, Physical Education, Recreation and Dance (AAHPERD)

19

Different instructors have different methods to help their students to improve. The capability of the instructors is also tested in their wits of being able to convince the students towards taking his/her instructions.

Which of the following psychomotor learning method is used when rewarding a student for completing tasks?

A) Physical - Reflex

B) Task - Reciprocal

C) Command - Direct

D) Contingency - Contract

20

The human's body weight is mostly determined by caloric intake and energy output. More consumption of food without any type of exercise may lead to obesity.

Which of the following is the best way to maintain weight?

A) Proper diet

B) Weight lifting

C) Aerobic exercise

D) Equalizing caloric intake relative to the output

21

Which of the following terms refers to the principle that states that every action has an equal and opposite reaction?

A) Inertia
B) Acceleration
C) Action/Reaction
D) Accelerated Motion

22

Regularly doing exercise can help the student maintain his body's condition. A healthy body is needed to perform well in sports and physical education.

Which of the following is not a physiological benefit of exercise?

A) Cardiac hypertrophy
B) Quicker recovery rate
C) Reducing mental tension
D) Improving muscle strength

23

Aerobic exercises can be categorized into many different areas, such as upper body aerobic exercises and lower body aerobic exercises. Some aerobic exercises also focus on body parts such as arms and legs.

Which of the following is developed by boat rowing?

A) Muscle force
B) Muscle volume
C) Muscle flexibility
D) Muscle endurance

24

US government is accepting immigrants from different places in the world. So, this diverse population can possibly cause conflict during classes.

Which of the following is not a strategy to assist in teaching students of diverse populations?

A) Station rotations
B) Peer to peer assisting
C) Group students by skill level
D) Have the less skilled students sit out certain activities

25

Which of the following statements best describes cardiorespiratory fitness?

A) It is the ability to create force constantly without feeling exhausted.

B) It is the ability to execute aerobic activity for an extended time.

C) It is the ability to do repetitive high-intensity muscle contractions.

D) It is the ability to perform vigorous physical activity without experiencing discomfort or stiffness.

26

Badminton games are more inclined to arms reach and reaction time aside from the required skills to play it, such as speed and technique. Simultaneously being able to react quickly, estimating the needed arm reach, and applying the appropriate technique can help the student to return the shuttlecock more often.

Which of the following is an overhead badminton stroke used to hit a forehand-like overhead stroke that is on the backhand side of the body?

A) Overhead shot

B) Lifted-arm shot

C) Underhand shuttle

D) Around-the-head shot

27

An average diet consists of meat, vegetables, and fruits. It is divided into portions and servings that satiate the average human body and gives it the energy it needs for the day.

Which of the following is an adequate diet that meets the nutritional needs of the body?

A) No more than 30% caloric intake from fats, no more than 15% caloric intake from proteins, and at least 55% caloric intake from carbohydrates

B) No more than 30 % caloric intake from fats, no more than 30% caloric intake from proteins, and at least 40% caloric intake from carbohydrates

C) No more than 30% caloric intake from fats, no more than 40% caloric intake from proteins, and at least 30% caloric intake from carbohydrates

D) No more than 30% caloric intake from fats, no more than 50 % caloric intake from proteins, and at least 20% caloric intake from carbohydrates

28

Which of the following part of the brain is responsible for refining skilled movements?

A) Pons

B) Cerebrum

C) Cerebellum

D) Medulla oblongata

29

Jumping requires an individual to jump off his two feet and land with both feet as well. This movement improves the legs' capacity to lift off the bodily weight for a short period using its power.

Which of the following health or skill-related component of fitness is developed by rope jumping?

A) Flexibility
B) Coordination
C) Muscle power
D) Muscle force

30

Soccer players can use their hands when inbounding the ball.

Which of the following is a soccer pass from the outside of the field near the end line to a position in front of the goal?

A) Chip
B) Cross
C) Settle
D) Through

31

Development is defined as the process of growth.

Which of the following type of development is exhibited by a student who enjoys doing physical activities and achieves a feeling of satisfaction?

A) Merit
B) Affective
C) Cognitive
D) Coordination

32

An appropriate hitting method must be used to return the shuttlecock to the other side of the court. A backhand or a forehand must be used accordingly to be able to return the shuttlecock accurately.

Which of the following is an overhead badminton stroke used to hit a fore-hand-like overhead stroke that is on the backhand side of the body?

A) Overhead shot
B) Underhanded shot
C) Down-the-line shot
D) Around-the-head shot

33

Class participation is vital for student learning since it helps students to express their ideas for others to understand them.

Which of the following involves changing the rules and equipment to fit the needs of students of different ability levels and physical development levels to enhance participation?

A) Quiz competition

B) Individual recitation

C) Activity modification

D) Heterogeneous grouping

34

Stationary objects refer to the objects that are at rest or not in motion.

Which of the following manipulative skills will likely to be developed by hitting a stationary object while stayin in a fixed position and then incorporating the movement?

A) Shaking

B) Striking

C) Dribbling

D) Trapping

35

A vision statement is a school's roadmap, indicating both what the school wants to become and guiding transformational initiatives by setting a defined direction for the school's growth.

What does an effective vision statement focus on?

A) Promotion of community diversity

B) High expectations for student learning

C) Teamwork between teachers and students

D) Continuous professional development of the school's teachers and other staff

CONTINUE ▶

36

The poor performance of a skill may result in the instructor intervening and prescribing a set of exercises to improve it. The instructor can evaluate the improvement of the student later in a given period.

Which of the following best accomplishes the evaluation of the poor performance of skill using process assessment?

A) Observing how long the skill is performed

B) Observing how fast the skill is performed

C) Observing how the skill is shown in a given time

D) Observing several attributes comprising the entire performance of a skill

37

The **muscles** of the body support the skeletal framework for us to be able to perform movements in daily life. Muscles can be improved through training and repeated extensive use.

Which of the following is the muscle's ability to repeatedly contract over a period of time?

A) Muscle force

B) Muscle strength

C) Muscle flexibility

D) Muscle endurance

38

A student's skill can be developed through proper training and exercise. Exercise helps develop the body to adapt through the changes that the proper training may require.

Which of the following refers to the coordinated movement of a person that aims to project him over an obstacle?

A) Hopping

B) Jumping

C) Leaping

D) Vaulting

39

Large range of sporting activities requires a set of skills. A **closed skill** is a skill in which the environment remains stable and the performer knows what to do and when to do it.

Which of the following about the closed skills is not correct?

A) Closed skills are habitual and follow set patterns from beginning to end.

B) The performers of the closed skills practice at a stable rate and they move to different rates as mastery is attained.

C) These skills are not affected by the environment and movements have a clear beginning and end.

D) They take place in an unpredictable environment and movements have to be continually adapted.

CONTINUE ▶

40

A woman has been exercising and running three miles several times a week for six weeks. She noticed that the muscles on her legs had gained more endurance; however, there has been a slight difference in the muscles' strength.

The runner's observation best demonstrates which of the following principles of exercise and sports training?

A) The principle of specificity
B) The principle of adaptation
C) The principle of progression
D) The principle of reversibility

41

The human body requires different needs to maintain its functionality. Necessary food must be provided to continue supplying energy to the body.

Which of the following is the most essential nutrient for the body that can be lethal in its absence in just a few days?

A) Water
B) Minerals
C) Vitamins
D) Carbohydrates

42

Overtraining means having a continuous intense training that does not allot enough recovery time.

Which of the following is not a byproduct of overtraining?

A) Imbalance between exercise and recovery
B) Training exceeds psychological and physiological capacity of a person
C) Negative effect on strength training
D) Always results in injury or illness

43

How many calories is required to have a negative energy balance in order to lose one pound per week?

A) 3,500
B) 2,500
C) 2,000
D) 1,500

44

Regular exercise helps the body maintain good physical capability. Muscles are less strained when doing a rigorous job around the house.

Which of the following is not a psychological benefit of exercise?

A) Improved appearance

B) Improved quality of life

C) Improved energy regulation

D) Improved sleeping patterns

45

Which of the following is the best fitness test to be used by a physical education teacher in assessing the fitness of students with disabilities?

A) President's Challenge

B) Brockport Physical Fitness Test

C) ActivityGram

D) Fitnessgram

46

Which of the following is the main reason for the detorioration of cartilage and bone at skeletal joints?

A) Excessive work out

B) Excessive body weight

C) Blood circulation problems

D) Lack of minerals such as calcium

47

A student's physical activity can develop his body's functionality, such as reaction speed, agility, strength, and endurance. Different exercises are prescribed depending on the goals of the student.

Which of the following conditions is not associated with a lack of physical activity?

A) Osteoporosis

B) Atherosclerosis

C) Longer life expectancy

D) Some types of diabetes

Fitness can be defined as the condition of being physically fit and healthy. Which of the following about the fitness is not correct?

A) The primary advantage of health-related physical fitness is to improve muscle strength.

B) The more you sweat during a workout, the more fat the body is burning" is not true. "No pain, no gain" is a workout myth.

C) Fitness is not merely the absence of disease or infirmity but it is a form of physical activity done primarily to improve one's health and physical fitness.

D) Maintaining physical fitness does not require major lifestyle changes. Fitness can be achieved by making small changes in what you eat and increasing your level of activity.

The governments treat the physical education curriculum as one of the major subjects. Because of the games that students participate, countries have focused their hearts and set their minds on competing with rival countries.

Which of the following is the most effective way to promote the physical education curriculum?

A) Relate physical education to humanitarianism

B) Relate physical education to economic change

C) Relate physical education to social communication

D) Relate physical education to the total educational process

Stretching is an exercise in which certain muscles or group of muscles are stretched or flexed so that the muscles' elasticity is improved and comfortable muscle tone is achieved.

Which of the following is not a type of stretching?

A) Isometric stretch

B) Muscular stretch

C) Relaxed stretch

D) Active stretch

Physical education teachers often adapt and modify activities to provide differentiated instruction to individuals or groups.

• Lowering the heights of nets.
• Changing the difficulty level of activities.
• Changing the size and surface type of playing areas.
• Shortening the durations of games or limiting participation times.
• Allowing students to choose among equipment of different sizes and weights.

Some strategies used in physical education classes to help all students maximize individual potential are given above. What are these strategies primarily used for?

A) Enhancing the challenging nature of games and activities.

B) Emphasizing the cooperative nature of games and activities.

C) Minimizing the need for students to develop competence.

D) Maximizing the inclusion and equal participation of students with diverse abilities.

52

During the term of President Eisenhower, the survey showed poor fitness levels of American youths. Thus, a 90 second-test that involved six simple movements compared US children to European children in terms of strength and flexibility.

Which of the following was the test used to discover the poor physical conditioning of youths in the Eisenhower Administration?

A) Spencer-Elias Tests
B) Kraus-Webber Tests
C) Selective Service Examination
D) Federal Agency Mandatory Test

53

A **protein diet** is necessary to ensure muscle growth and development. A skinny student can start with a higher-than-average protein diet to steadily increase the protein mass in his muscles.

Which of the following is the characteristics of a high protein diet?

A) High in cholesterol
B) High in saturated fats
C) Require vitamin and mineral supplements
D) All of the above

54

The affective domain is the intrapersonal range of our emotions, feelings, and attitude that we use to deal with other people. This domain includes the manner that we use them to interact and deal with different situations.

Which of the following is not a method to evaluate the affective domain?

A) Adams Prosocial Inventory
B) Blanchard Behavior Rating Scale
C) Crowell Personal Distance Scale
D) McCloy's Prosocial Behavior Scale

55

Professional sports organizations sponsor events for the students who can compete with other prominent sports players and enthusiasts. These organizations are established to promote, protect, and maintain the healthy competition between students.

Which of the following organizations works with the legislature?

A) Amateur Athletic Union
B) American College of Sports Medicine
C) Association for Intercollegiate Athletics for Women
D) American Alliance for Health, Physical Education, Recreation and Dance

Which of the following would be the most appropriate ruling when two opposing players hit the volleyball net at the same time?

A) Sideout

B) Replay

C) Substitution

D) No gain/loss point

The concept of progression for an exercise lets the body get used to a gradual increase in the difficulty of the regimen. It reduces the risk of injury and can steadily build the body's capability and endurance.

Which of the following applies to the concept of progression?

A) Beginning a stretching program every day

B) Beginning a stretching program with 3 sets of reps

C) Beginning a stretching program with ballistic stretching

D) Beginning a stretching program holding stretches for 15 seconds and work up to holding stretches for 60 seconds

58

Basketball is a popular sport that involves a team of 5 (for both sides) to play an official match. It requires the players to dribble the ball using their hands and shoot it through the hoop of the ring to score.

Which of the following can be done to improve free-throw shooting in basketball?

A) Strength training

B) Increase releasing speed

C) Increase vertical path of the ball

D) Develop height release and hitting the box

59

Cooper's Formula is a physical fitness formula used to determine the target heart rate of a student when he/she is reaching a range of percentage of his/her heart rate while doing aerobic exercises.

Which of the following is the target heart rate for a 15-year-old student?

A) 120-153 beats per minute

B) 123-164 beats per minute

C) 130-169 beats per minute

D) 141-174 beats per minute

60

Exercise is often described as training and exertion of the lungs, muscles, and heart. Even moderate exercise reduces the risk of heart disease, diabetes, hypertension, and obesity because exercise is the silver bullet for a better quality of life.

Which of the following about the exercise is not correct?

A) Frequency, duration, intensity, and kind of exercises are important points to consider for a desirable level of fitness.

B) Exercise reduces the risk of diabetes and cardiac injury during a heart attack. It also increases bone mass.

C) Exercise is one of several components of a lifestyle that leads to wellness. Weight loss should be the main reason for people to exercise.

D) There are plenty of exercises you can do at home or outdoors using your own body weight and gravity. Some examples include jumping jacks, push-ups, and sit-ups.

61

Stress is a mental or physical strain on a person that can result in both positive and negative aspects. Sleeplessness or being hyperactive can be signs of stress.

Which of the following is not a sign of stress?

A) Insomnia

B) Irritability

C) Assertiveness

D) Stomach problems

A **cardio-respiratory assessment** is a type of assessment test used to determine the levels of heart rate and oxygen intake of a student. It includes the capability of the heart and lungs to endure different types of exercises and their period.

Which of the following cannot be predicted from the data obtained from such a test?

A) Motivation
B) Running ability
C) Natural fat storage
D) Functional aerobic capacity

The primary mission of **AAHPERD** is to motivate people of all ages and sizes to achieve and maintain physical fitness, health, and well-being.

Which of the following is not established by the AAHPER Fitness Conferences established in 1956?

A) The President's Citizens' Advisory Committee
B) The President's Council on Youth Fitness
C) The President's Council on Mental Fitness
D) All of the above

CONTINUE ▶

64

Badminton is a racquet sport played using racquets to hit a shuttlecock across a net.

In badminton, which of the following would be the most critical element on a ready position?

A) Bending knees

B) Putting feet together

C) Holding the racket up

D) Holding the racket sidewards

65

Motor learning and safety for potentially injurious sports were best promoted by which of the following practice alternatives?

A) Partial part

B) Whole part

C) Progressive part

D) Distributed part

66

A student must be prescribed with a goal for his physical education classes to develop his body and to obtain a certain type of self-satisfaction. Learning the proper technique as the basics of exercise can be helpful in the long run.

Which of the following technique must be learned first to enhance skill and strategy performance for striking or throwing objects, for catching or collecting objects, and for carrying and propelling objects?

A) Offense

B) Defense

C) Controlling objects

D) Extensive playing hours

CONTINUE ▶

67

Locomotor movements refer to the movements that travel through space or carry weight from one location to another while a **non-locomotor** movement refers to a movement of a person at stationary.

Which of the following about locomotor and nonlocomotor skills is incorrect?

A) Bending is a locomotor skill which restricts movement around a joint where two body parts meet.

B) Hopping is a locomotor skill that uses the same foot to take off from a surface and land.

C) Dodging is a nonlocomotor skill that involves a sharp change of direction from one's original line of movement.

D) None of the above

68

The British tradition of fair play is a fair treatment of people without cheating or being dishonest.

Which of the following is the goal of educators to students in using the British tradition of fair play in physical education programs?

A) Sportsmanship

B) Self-assessment

C) Self-confidence

D) Teamwork

69

Vertical jump shows the potential of the legs to hold the upper body and the strength in the joints of the legs.

Which of the following components does vertical jump assess when performed?

A) Power
B) Agility
C) Balance
D) Stamina

70

In response to a heavy loading session, which of the following exercises requires the longets recovery time for the stressed muscle groups?

A) Knee extension
B) Bench press
C) Front squat
D) Dumbbell fly

71

A student was so frustrated since he has not get the gold medal in the swimming competition. His coach told him that he was so sorry to see him disappointed besides doing all the training.

Why is the coach's response appropriate?

A) It provides an objective overview.
B) It affirms that the student set a goal and worked hard.
C) It shows appreciation for the student's performance.
D) It emphasizes the coach's knowledge of his student's span of practice.

72

Which of the following organizations promotes and supports leadership, research, education, and best practices that support creative, healthy, and active lifestyles of physical education teachers to introduce their programs in more population?

A) Trail Association
B) Department of Education
C) Professional Accomplished Practices
D) Society of Health and Physical Educators

73

A toddler is a child who is 12 to 36 months old. The toddler years are a time of great cognitive, emotional and social development. The word is derived from "to toddle," which means to hobble, like a child of this age.

Which of the following is the main reason that toddlers learn to run after several months of learning to walk?

A) Running is more stable and requires higher body mass.

B) Running requires softer muscles which develop later on a toddler.

C) Running involves supporting body weight in all phases and thus requires additional strength.

D) Running is less stable and requires the development of greater motor control and coordination.

74

A blister is a painful swelling on the skin, often filled with a watery liquid, caused by a burn or by rubbing against something.

Which of the following precautions should be taken into consideration to prevent blisters in hiking?

A) Keeping hydrated before hiking

B) Warming up on cold days of hiking

C) Wearing socks that air cannot damp onto the skin

D) Wearing sturdy, proper-fitting hiking shoes that have been broken in

75

Which of the following is the purpose of having a correct racing posture when an athlete is a swimmer, a cyclist of a downhill skier?

A) The correct racing posture minimizes the effect of propulsion.

B) The correct racing posture minimizes the effect of lift.

C) The correct racing posture minimizes the effect of gravity.

D) The correct racing posture minimizes the effect of drag.

76

The main purpose of aerobic endurance training is to enhance and preserve the fitness of the cardiovacscular system of the body. Aerobic endurance training has different types.

Which of the following is not one of the aerobic endurance training exercises.

A) Pace

B) Repetition

C) Sequencing

D) Slow distance training

77

School districts supply teachers with curriculum and necessary documents.

Why should teachers still prepare annual and unit plans?

A) It is not necessary to develop annual and unit plans.

B) All school districts force teachers to write and submit annual and unit plans.

C) While preparing annual and unit plans by their own, teachers better understand what to teach.

D) Textbooks may not address all required standards, and teachers might have to supplement the curriculum.

78

The balance beam is a cube/rectangular artistic gymnastics apparatus.

Which of the following is the main advantage of female adolescents in showing greater motor control on a balance beam than male adolescents?

A) Shorter legs and feet

B) Lighter body weight

C) Lower center of gravity

D) Greater body density relative to overall body composition

## 79

The 5 components of physical fitness are often used in school systems, health clubs and fitness centers to measure how in shape the people are truly in.

What are the 5 components of physical education?

A) Muscular strength, muscular endurance, flexibility, body composition, muscular density

B) Muscular strength, flexibilty, verticle jump, body composition, cardiovascular endurance

C) Muscular strength, muscular endurance, cardiovascular endurance, flexibility, body composition

D) Muscular strength, cardiovascular strength, cardiovascular endurance, flexibility, verticle jump

## 80

Cognitive thinking refers to the use of mental activities and skills to perform tasks such as learning, reasoning, understanding, remembering and paying attention.

In order to determine a student's cognitive understanding of the mechanics of a particular skill, which of the following methods would be the most effective?

A) Observe the student doing the skill.

B) Prepare a pen and paper examination.

C) Allow the student to evaluate her skill development.

D) Listen to the student while she is teaching the skill to another student.

81

According to **the progressive overload principle**, in order for a muscle to grow, strength to be gained, performance to increase, or for any similar improvement to occur, the human body must be forced to adapt to a tension that is above and beyond what it has previously experienced.

An athlete is designing a variable-resistance training program to develop muscular endurance rather than strength. Which of the following best describes the application of the principle of progressive overload?

A) Gradually increasing the number of repetitions of resistance exercises

B) Increasing the duration of rest intervals on one exercise over time

C) Decreasing the training time for each exercise

D) Increasing the weight that the muscles can hold

82

A team of physical education teachers meet regularly to review the scope of the content across grade levels.

Which of the following is the major benefit of this practice?

A) It ensures the overall continuity of the physical education curriculum and skill instruction.

B) It promotes flexible instructional pacing for physical education content and skills.

C) It addresses the individual learning needs of students at varying developmental stages.

D) It streamlines the process of curriculum planning and evaluation.

83

An opportunity to reflect on what should students learn and they need to improve is best allowed by which of the following instructional models?

A) Self-reviewing

B) Group studying

C) Cooperative learning

D) Weekly reading and solving problems

84

Which of the following is the benefit of setting an activity on students that evaluate their heart rate after walking, jogging and sprinting with slow, medium or fast pace?

A) Explaining the difference between aerobic and anaerobic activities

B) Helping student to identify their normal heart rate

C) Teaching student in calculating respiration rates during aerobic activity

D) Introducing students to basic cardio-respiratory fitness principles in the context of a physical activity

85

Fatigue is described as severe tiredness which is normally a result of physical or mental exertion.

Which of the following will result in the student to feel fatigue?

A) Dehydration

B) Sleep deprivation

C) Depleted creatine phosphate

D) Depleted muscle glycogen

86

Motor Behavior is a program in exercise science that prepares students to enter physical or occupational therapy or other related professional schools.

Which of the following is being integrated into motor behaviors when the ability to time movements to intercept a moving object is dependent?

A) Air resistance and the object's weight

B) Source of the force and the object's weight

C) Momentum and relative positions of the object

D) Sensory information about the speed and direction of the object

87

Periodization is the systematic manipulation of the of the acute variables of training over a particular time that possibly ranges from days to years. Early eastern countries developed the original concept of periodization to improve the effectiveness of the adaptation of athletes to resistance training which usually revolves around the athletes' competitive calendar for them to be at their competitive peak for competition.

Which fo the following is the main idea behind periodization?

A) Changing the training type

B) Decrease resistance by 5%

C) Varying training intensity and volume

D) Exercising the appropriate muscles

88

Which of the following should a skills-based approach fitness education program for middle and high school students provide?

A) A discussion on how the environment affects fitness

B) Sufficient practice opportunities in one or two movement form to develop high levels of proficiency in those areas

C) List of available places that can provide adequate resources for the fitness program they specifically need.

D) The knowledge and strategies that are essential for improving fitness and maintaining lifelong physical activity

89

Building bigger and stronger biceps have always been desired by men throughout the world. The standing barbell curl is an effective isolation exercise that works your bicep muscles, along with training the muscles in the shoulders and the forearms.

Which of the following best describes the generation of force during a standing barbell curl by a muscle group?

A) The generation of force varies throughout the full range of motion.

B) The generation of force remains constant throughout the full range of motion.

C) The maximal force-development capacity should remain constant as the weight is lifted above waist-level.

D) There should be no maximal force-development as the weight is lifted above waist-level.

90

In order to develop good attitude in children about their body composition and body image, which of the following will be the best approach?

A) Teaching children the different diets and eating patterns

B) Asking children to determine their body mass index and explain it

C) Instructing children to observe their families' eating habit and adapt them

D) Emphasizing that individuals come in a variety of sizes and shapes within a range of healthy body weights

Breaststroke is a swimming technique in which the swimmer's face is in the water and the arms move in a large motion from front to back as the feet kick outward.

Which of the following are the two common mistakes demonstrated by novice swimmers who are just learning the breaststroke?

A) Moving the arms too fast; Carrying the arms too high in the recovery

B) Pulling the arms back too far; Improper timing between movements of the legs and the arms

C) Moving the arms too fast; Pulling the arms back too far

D) Failure to relax; Improper timing between movements of the legs and the arms

CRAWL: A form of locomotion where the person moves in a prone position with the body resting on or close to the ground or on the hands and knees.

CREEP: A slightly more advanced form of locomotion in which the person moves on the hands and knees.

WALK: A form of locomotion in which body weight is transferred alternately from the ball (toe) of one foot to the heel of the other. At times one foot is on the ground and during a brief phase, both feet are on the ground.

RUN: A form of locomotion much like the walk except that the tempo and body lean may differ. At times one foot is on the ground and during a brief phase both feet are off the ground.

Locomotor skills are the skills that utilize the feet and that propels an individual from one place to another.

How many of the locomotor skills given above are defined correctly?

A) 1

B) 2

C) 3

D) 4

93

The Whole School, Whole Community, Whole Child or WSCC model incorporates the components CSH and the principles of ASCD's (Association for Supervision and Curriculum Development) whole child approach to strengthen a unified and collaborative approach to learning and health.

Which of the following does WSCC model include?

A) Nutrition and environment services
B) Comprehensive school health education
C) Physical education and physical activity
D) All of the above

94

Norm-referenced tests report whether test takers performed better or worse than a hypothetical average student, which is determined by comparing scores against the performance results of a statistically selected group of test takers, typically of the same age or grade level, who have already taken the exam.

In assessing physical education students, which of the following should be mostly ensured when using a standardized, norm-referenced assessment software?

A) The test should include standardized essay and identification problems.
B) Test items should correspond to specific levels of the psychomotor taxonomy.
C) The demographic characteristics of the norm group should be similar to those of the group being tested.
D) The difficulty of the questions should be arranged according to the lowest performing student.

Adolescence typically describes the years between ages 13 and 19. It can be considered the transitional stage from childhood to adulthood. However, it can start earlier, during the preteen years.

In the adolescent stage of human growth and development, which of the following cognitive mile-stones can be best associated?

A) Readiness to conform to the spoken word

B) Having short attention span and easily distracted

C) Building interest in abstract ideas and the process of thinking itself

D) Learning to take intentions into account in judging the behaviors of others

Heat exhaustion is a condition whose symptoms may include heavy sweating and a rapid pulse as a result of your body overheating.

A student suddenly fell to the ground while playing outdoor fun games activities. As an initial response, the teacher moved the student into a shady area and check signs of heat exhaustion. Which of the following should be the teacher's next step?

A) Sprinkle water on student's face

B) Give the student sips of water or a sports drink

C) Call the ambulance and do not move the student

D) Cover the student with a light blanket and elevate his or feet

Which of the following about physical activity, physical education, and school sport is not correct?

A) Physical Activity is a broad term referring to all bodily movement that uses energy.

B) School Sport is the structured learning that takes place beyond the curriculum within school settings.

C) Physical Education is the planned, progressive learning that takes place in the school curriculum and it is delivered to all students.

D) PE involves "learning to move" (becoming more physically competent) and does not involve 'moving to learn' (learning through movement such as cooperating with others).

Developmental psychology is concerned with the scientific understanding of age-related changes in experience and behavior, not only in children but throughout the lifespan.

Which of the following best explains the role of playing in young children's growth and development according to the principles of developmental psychology?

A) Play allows children to observe other children's behavior towards others

B) Play allows children to understand the environment and issues to be taken

C) Play allows children to try out and test new physical, cognitive, and social behaviors, which then become part of their working memory

D) Play provides important information about gender roles, children with limited opportunities to play often experience delayed development of gender identity

Digital media refers to audio, video, and photo content that has been encoded while word processing is the phrase used to describe using a computer to create, edit, and print documents.

A teacher asks his 7th-grade students to document their assessment of own fitness through digital media and word processing. Which of the following should a teacher suggest to protect the privacy of the students' work?

A) Open their post for public view.

B) Instruct students to gather information through the Internet.

C) Post their project on a secured website for the teacher to review.

D) Share their post in public view and name the author as anonymous.

Dribbling in soccer is the way in which soccer players advance the ball with their feet.

Which of the following is the most suitable technique when a soccer coach is trying to emphasize players on points when dribbling a soccer ball?

A) Keeping the ball in straight motion without going out in any direction

B) Using a running motion to travel and delivering a series of taps to the ball with the foot

C) Keeping eye on the direction of the motion of the ball

D) Moving at a speed faster than a walk and keeping the ball within two to four feet of the body

SECTION 5 - PHYSICAL EDUCATION

#	Answer	Topic	Subtopic	#	Answer	Topic	Subtopic	#	Answer	Topic	Subtopic	#	Answer	Topic	Subtopic
1	D	TB	S1	26	D	TB	S2	51	D	TB	S7	76	C	TB	S4
2	C	TB	S4	27	A	TB	S6	52	B	TB	S5	77	D	TB	S5
3	A	TB	S7	28	C	TB	S2	53	D	TB	S4	78	C	TB	S2
4	C	TB	S3	29	B	TB	S4	54	D	TB	S5	79	C	TB	S4
5	B	TB	S6	30	B	TB	S2	55	D	TB	S7	80	D	TB	S2
6	D	TB	S5	31	B	TB	S2	56	B	TB	S3	81	A	TB	S2
7	C	TB	S3	32	D	TB	S3	57	D	TB	S2	82	A	TB	S6
8	B	TB	S2	33	C	TB	S6	58	C	TB	S2	83	C	TB	S1
9	C	TB	S2	34	B	TB	S3	59	B	TB	S4	84	D	TB	S1
10	A	TB	S1	35	B	TB	S2	60	C	TB	S4	85	D	TB	S4
11	B	TB	S4	36	D	TB	S5	61	C	TB	S4	86	D	TB	S2
12	B	TB	S1	37	D	TB	S4	62	C	TB	S4	87	C	TB	S4
13	C	TB	S2	38	D	TB	S2	63	C	TB	S7	88	D	TB	S2
14	D	TB	S4	39	D	TB	S3	64	C	TB	S3	89	A	TB	S3
15	D	TB	S3	40	A	TB	S4	65	C	TB	S1	90	D	TB	S3
16	A	TB	S3	41	A	TB	S4	66	C	TB	S3	91	B	TB	S3
17	D	TB	S4	42	D	TB	S4	67	A	TB	S4	92	D	TB	S4
18	D	TB	S6	43	A	TB	S3	68	A	TB	S2	93	D	TB	S3
19	D	TB	S1	44	D	TB	S4	69	A	TB	S5	94	C	TB	S2
20	D	TB	S4	45	B	TB	S1	70	C	TB	S4	95	C	TB	S2
21	C	TB	S6	46	B	TB	S4	71	B	TB	S3	96	B	TB	S1
22	C	TB	S4	47	C	TB	S2	72	D	TB	S3	97	D	TB	S1
23	D	TB	S4	48	B	TB	S4	73	D	TB	S2	98	C	TB	S2
24	D	TB	S1	49	D	TB	S1	74	D	TB	S3	99	C	TB	S3
25	B	TB	S4	50	B	TB	S4	75	D	TB	S3	100	B	TB	S3

Topics & Subtopics

Code	Description	Code	Description
SB1	Planning Instruction	SB5	Student Assessment
SB2	Student Growth & Development	SB6	Communication, Collaboration & Technology
SB3	Planning Activities	SB7	Management & Motivation
SB4	Health-Related Physical Fitness	TB	Physical Education

172

CONTINUE ▶

TEST DIRECTION

Read the questions carefully and then choose the ONE best answer to each question.

Be sure to allocate your time carefully so you are able to complete the entire test within the testing session. You may go back and review your answers at any time.

You may use any available space in your test booklet for scratch work.

Questions in this booklet are not actual test questions but they are the samples for commonly asked questions.

This test aims to cover all topics which may appear on the actual test. However some topics may not be covered.

Studying this booklet will be preparing you for the actual test. It will not guarantee improving your test score but it will help you pass your exam on the first attempt.

Some useful tips for answering multiple choice questions;

- Start with the questions that you can easily answer.

- Underline the keywords in the question.

- Be sure to read all the choices given.

- Watch for keywords such as NOT, always, only, all, never, completely.

- Do not forget to answer every question.

1

In the United States market, some public policies require the manufacturers to add vitamins and minerals on cereals and milk that are sold.

Which of the following is the primary purpose of these public policies?

A) To extend the shelf life of food products.

B) To increase the food product's nutrient value.

C) To protect the public from illnesses that can be derived from food

D) To minimize the development of food intolerance conditions.

2

Several studies show that lack of sleep is correlatead with diabetes, heart disease, immune system suppression.

Which of the following groups is at most risk of having the health concerns mentioned above?

A) High socioeconomic status groups

B) Low socioeconomic status groups

C) Student working atleast 20 hours per week

D) Employees working atleast 40 hours per week

3

Fungal diseases, like athlete's foot and ringworms, are prevented by which of the following?

A) Maintaining a balanced diet and exercising regularly

B) Washing hands carefully and avoiding direct contact with infected people

C) Cooking animal food thoroughly and avoiding contaminated water

D) Practicing good personal hygiene and using dry clothes

4

The immune system is the defense system of the body that contains cells categorized as lymphocytes, monocytes, and neutrophils.

In which of the following do these cells move throughout the body?

A) The nutrients of the digestive system

B) The fluids of the circulatory and lymphatic systems

C) The neurotransmitters of the nervous system

D) The hormones of the reproductive and endocrine systems

CONTINUE ▶

Violence prevention programs should be established between which of the following?

A) Home and District

B) School and County

C) School, Home and State

D) School, Home and Community

Anxiety is a feeling of nervousness, or worry that generally occurs in the absence of an impending threat. It is a natural reaction to stress, so it can be helpful at times by making you more alert and ready for action.

Which of the following personal strategies would be the most effective for mitigating feelings of generalized anxiety and stress?

A) Ignoring distressing things in life hoping that they will end.

B) Expressing thoughts to a friend or family member frequently.

C) Redirecting attention and energy to a pleasant activity such as playing a game.

D) Challenging to tackle a difficult task that has been avoided before.

7

Primary prevention focuses on good populations, and it is implemented before disease occurs.

Which of the following about primary prevention is not correct?

A) Primary prevention aims to prevent disease or health problems before exposure or onset of illness.

B) Immunization is an example of primary prevention, and the primary objective of immunization programs is to cure the infection.

C) Law enforcement to ban or control the use of unhealthy or hazardous products is an example of primary prevention.

D) Education about healthy and safe habits, altering unhealthy or unsafe behaviors that can lead to disease or injury is an example of primary prevention.

8

The cholesterol content of baked desserts can be manipulated by modifying certain ingredients.

Among the ingredients commonly used in baking, which of the following can reduce cholesterol content effectively?

A) Using egg whites instead of whole eggs.

B) Using shortening instead of cooking oil.

C) Using raw sugar instead of refined sugar.

D) Using all-purpose flour instead of whole wheat flour.

9

In an emergency, which of the following options is the most practical way to guarantee that an accident victim gets a medical response immediately?

A) Calling 911 on the phone.

B) Calling the nearest hospital.

C) Contacting the office of the victim's chief care physician.

D) Communicating with a medical expert with relevant medication skills.

10

Marga, after receiving a clean health bill from both her doctor and dentist, was instructed to have regularly scheduled check-ups, both medical and dental.

Which of the following statements best describes the reason for the regular check-ups?

A) To monitor her gain of weight to prevent her from becoming obese.

B) To prevent an increase in the cost of her health insurance premiums.

C) To detect any health problems that are developing to prevent it from advancing any further.

D) If there are any injuries sustained during daily exercise routines, these injuries can be treated immediately, and not escalate any further.

11

Which of the following minerals are young children and women aged 20 to 35 years old most likely be deficient of?

A) Calcium (Ca)

B) Iron (Fe)

C) Sodium (Na)

D) Potassium (K)

12

Which of the following term is not defined correctly?

A) Pathology is the study of the cause of disease

B) Life expectancy is from birth, how long you are expected to live.

C) Total number of disease cases in a population is called as Prevalence

D) Morbidity is a public health term to describe the frequency of deaths produced by a disease or other condition

13

Fetal alcohol syndrome is a condition in children that results from alcohol consumption or exposure during a woman's pregnancy. This disorder is related to which of the following?

A) Developmental disabilities: A group of conditions due to an impairment in physical, learning, language, or behavior areas.

B) Hepatitis: An inflammation of the liver which is highly contagious.

C) Anemia: A condition in which the blood doesn't have enough healthy red blood cells.

D) Leukemia: A cancer of blood-forming tissues, hindering the ability of the body to fight infection.

14

According to health experts, when an individual has a small chance of acting on its own, he or she may acquire a deep-seated need for control.

Once this need is achieved through excessive control over one's body, it becomes a coping response that is vital in the development of which of the following disorders?

A) Schizophrenia

B) Asperger's syndrome

C) Anorexia or bulimia nervosa

D) Bipolar or manic-depressive disorder

15

In 1928, Alexander Fleming, a Professor of Bacteriology at St. Mary's Hospital in London, accidentally discovered penicillin. **Penicillins** are a group of drugs that attack a wide variety of bacteria by interfering with the bacterial cell walls.

Which of the following diseases is treated by using penicillin?

A) Athlete's Foot: A fungal infection, also called tinea pedis, that usually begins between the toes.

B) Pneumonia: A respiratory infection that inflames the air sacs in one or both lungs.

C) Genital Herpes: A common, highly contagious sexually transmitted disease (STD) caused by infection by the herpes simplex virus type 2 (HSV-2).

D) Trichinosis: An infection caused by the roundworm Trichinella spiralis or another Trichinella species.

16

Consuming large amounts of foods and drinks containing sugar can cause various health problems on children such as obesity. Aside from sugar, adding phosphorous to a soda can also be harmful to children's health.

Which of the following explains the negative effect of phosphorous?

A) The metabolism of fat-soluble vitamins is prevented by phosphorus.

B) Calcium is drawn out of bones that are still developing since phosphorus binds with calcium.

C) Compared with adult kidneys, phosphorus can remain in a child's immature kidneys.

D) Formation of new cells with the help of water-soluble vitamins can be interfered by phosphorus.

17

The Center for Disease Control Prevention (CDC) developed a framework known as the Whole School, Whole Community, Whole Child (WSCC) model, to address health in schools. WSCC has ten components.

Which of the following components considers the school's physical and aesthetic surroundings?

A) Nutrition services

B) Emotional climate

C) Physical environment

D) Psychological and social services

18

Several factors affect a person's development concerning physical health and nutritional habits. These factors may be positive or negative.

Which of the following would have the most significant positive influence on a person's physical health and nutritional habits?

A) Joining extracurricular activities after school or work.

B) Being exposed in an environment that practices and values health habits.

C) Gaining knowledge about food preparation from watching cooking shows.

D) Gathering information about the benefits of exercise from sources like magazine articles.

19

Lea, an 18-year old girl, is experiencing compulsive eating in large amounts.

Which of the following conditions does Lea most likely have?

A) Bulimia nervosa

B) Binge eating disorder

C) Orthorexia Nervosa

D) Anorexia nervosa

20

A girl is attempting to build a Barbie House out of legos. After several barbie houses fall over, the girl moves along to play with a Barbie Baby.

Which of the following internal ability does this behavior reflect?

A) Playing with a variety of toys

B) Modifying emotional responses

C) Determining learning strengths

D) Continuing with a task under pressure

CONTINUE ▶

21

Ephedra is an herb that may stimulate the heart, lungs or the nervouse system due to the ephedrine it contains. It is usually added to some herbal supplements, however, an increased risk for a particular health problem has been shown associated with the use of Ephedra.

Which of the following health problem is being referred in the statement given above?

A) Brain damage

B) Cardiac arrest

C) Stomach cancer

D) Congenital disabilities

22

In the last 20 years, there has been an increase in Type 2 diabetes.

Which of the following is the primary cause of this increase?

A) The increase in adults having substance abuse.

B) The increase in the survival rates of people with diabetes.

C) The increase in adults and children having unhealthy diet and bad exercise habits.

D) The increase in individuals from the population susceptible to Type 2 diabetes.

23

Which of the following is the leading cause of death for both men and women in the U.S. and in the world?

A) Cancer

B) HIV or AIDS

C) Cardiovascular disease

D) Accidents and violence-related events

24

Which of the following statements best describes the essential amino acids?

A) These are important constituents of fats, carbohydrates, and proteins.

B) These are the amino acids that occur naturally and are primarily responsible for fighting infections.

C) These are the amino acids considered as high-energy nutrients for promoting growth and development.

D) These are the amino acids needed for the synthesis of proteins but mostly cannot be produced by the body.

Human actions towards the environment have advantages and disadvantages. An example of its disadvantages is acid rain.

Which of the following human activities is the primary source of the acid rains?

A) The burning of solid wastes.

B) Use of wood stoves for heating homes.

C) Fossil fuels being incenerated in smelters, mills, and power plants.

D) The use of substances in manufacturing that emit radiation.

A **doctor** is a person skilled in the field of medicine and trained and licensed to cure sick and injured people.

Which of the following types of doctor primarily serves the elderly community?

A) Obstetrician

B) Pediatrician

C) Geriatrician

D) Toxicologist

27

The CDC or the Centers for Disease Control and Prevention is a national health facility that aims to preserve public health and security through the control and prevention of disease, injury, and disability.

According to CDC, which of the following is included in the top five causes of death for people aged 15 to 19?

A) Anemia
B) Diabetes
C) Pneumonia
D) Unintentional injuries

28

What biomolecule is converted into glucose by muscle cells which is also a multi-branched polysaccharide of glucose that serves as a storage of energy in animals, fungi, and humans?

A) Muscle glycogen
B) High triglycerides
C) Free fatty acids
D) Creatine phosphate

29

Which of the following minerals should adolescents that reached puberty, need to increase their intake compared with prepubescent girls?

A) Iodine (I)
B) Iron (Fe)
C) Zinc (Zn)
D) Phosphorus (Ph)

CONTINUE ▶

30

Blood screening is done to detect signs of infection to reduce the possible risks and treat the disease more efficiently. This method is most significant in preventing which of the following?

A) Encephalitis: An inflammation of the brain tissue.

B) Meningitis: An inflammation of the protective membranes covering the brain and spinal cord.

C) Hepatitis B: A serious infection of the liver which increases the risk of developing liver failure, liver cancer or cirrhosis

D) West Nile Virus: A virus spread by mosquitoes which is the leading cause of mosquito-borne disease in the continental United States

31

Insomnia is a disease which is also known as sleeplessness. It is a sleep disorder which is caused by psychiatric and medical conditions, unhealthy sleep habits, specific substances, and certain biological factors that makes it difficult to fall asleep.

People with sleeplessness can have difficulty falling asleep, waking up often during the night and having trouble going back to sleep again.

Which of the following stress management techniques would be effective for an individual suffering from insomnia?

A) An exercise program

B) Progressive relaxation

C) Stress inoculation

D) Guided imagery

32

There are ten main systems in the human body, and each has different roles.

Which of the following system serves as the first line of defense of the body against infection?

A) Immune system

B) Lymphatic system

C) Respiratory system

D) Integumentary system

33

Prozac is an antidepressant which is also known as fluoxetine. It is mainly used to treat major depression, panic disorder, and obsessive-compulsive disorder.

Which of the following neurotransmitters (chemical substance which is released at the end of a nerve after the arrival of an impulse) is most affected by the antidepressant Prozac?

A) Cortisol

B) Serotonin

C) Adrenaline

D) Epinephrine

34

Children are more susceptive to different types of diseases, such as measles, tetanus, chicken pox, polio, and diphtheria because their organ systems are still developing.

Which of the following statements is a common characteristic of the diseases mentioned above?

A) All diseases are caused by bacteria.

B) All diseases affect the circulatory system.

C) All diseases can be prevented by using vaccines.

D) All diseases have a significant impact on the immune system.

35

Human development is a lifetime process of change. Throughout this procedure, an individual acquires values and attitudes that supervise understanding, choices, and relationships.

According to studies, which of the following factors has the most substantial positive impact on the emotional health and wellness of older adults?

A) Taking care of grandchildren or any other young relative.

B) Trying different lifestyles and self-refining activities.

C) Maintaining closer ties with family and friends.

D) Working full time again after the well passed retirement years.

36

Which of the following is the reason why adolescents that experienced growth are physically uncoordinated?

A) Growth rate of different parts of the musculoskeletal system are a different.

B) Fast fluctuations in metabolic processes result from the hormonal imbalances due to puberty.

C) The fast growth of the brain and the nervous system causes a lack of focus and concentration.

D) Changes in the middle ear that occur late in adolescence is usually associated with the development of kinesthetic sense.

37

Which of the following about the minerals is not correct?

A) Exposure to Chromium VI causes the highest risk of cancer.

B) Calcium, potassium, and sodium are classified as Catecholamines.

C) Iodine deficiency can result in permanent mental retardation.

D) Minerals are the nutrients from the soil that are found in foods.

38

The ecosystem can be preserved optimally by which of the following scenarios given below?

A) The alteration of the ecosystem's territorial space only.

B) Recycling and reusing all resources and maintaining the energy level within the ecosystem constant.

C) Obtaining natural resources from the ecosystem at a rate which will support human needs.

D) The non-living components of the ecosystem are regarded as not important and replaceable; unlike the living components, the plants and animals, which are protected.

39

Tay-Sachs disease is a genetic disorder that destroys the nerve cells in the brain and spinal cord. This disease is most prevalent in which of the following populations?

A) Asians

B) European Jews

C) North Americans

D) South Americans

40

Tertiary Prevention's goal is to slow the progression of diseases and reduce the complications.

Which of the following about tertiary prevention is not correct?

A) Tertiary prevention aims to detect a disease in its earliest stages, before symptoms appear.

B) The treatments of tertiary prevention can include several professionals including doctor, medical specialist, occupational therapist, physiotherapist and etc.

C) Helping people handle complex health problems and injuries to improve quality of life and their life expectancy is a goal of tertiary prevention.

D) Tertiary prevention refers to treating the disease like arthritis, asthma, heart disease, cancer and diabetes and providing rehabilitation for people who are already affected by a disease.

41

Which of the following does a family system, the building block of the society, contribute to?

A) Provide developmental experiences for all members.

B) Provide a stable physical environment for all members.

C) Meet physical and emotional needs of individuals.

D) Meet educational and social needs of individuals.

42

Rubella is a viral infection known for its characteristic red rash. Although considered a relatively mild disease, it can pose a serious threat to several people.

Which of the following is the most critical reason for immunization against rubella?

A) A person infected by rubella can develop a case of meningitis or encephalitis that can result in death.

B) An elderly adult who incurred rubella as a child is at risk of acquiring a painful and debilitating case of shingles.

C) A pregnant woman who incurs rubella during the first trimester of her pregnancy can give birth to an infant with severe congenital disabilities.

D) A baby who contracts rubella is at risk of permanent paralysis resulting from nervous and muscular degradation in the arms and legs.

43

Schizophrenia is a long-term mental condition that affects how a person thinks, feels, and behaves. People with schizophrenia may seem like they have lost touch with reality.

At which of the following age brackets are people most likely diagnosed with schizophrenia?

A) As a child
B) Around college age
C) During adolescence
D) In older adulthood

44

Alzheimer's disease is an irreversible, chronic brain disorder that slowly destroys thinking and memory skills, and eventually the ability to do the simplest tasks. It is the most common cause of dementia among adults.

Which of the following is considered a risk factor linked with the onset of Alzheimer's Early retirement disease?

A) Gain of weight
B) Lack of exercise
C) Early retirement
D) High consumption of green vegetables

45

A woman's body undergoes a hormonal process, known as the **menstrual cycle**, for the preparation of a possible pregnancy.

On average, after how many days does the ovulation phase of the menstrual cycle occur again?

A) 3 to 5 days

B) 7 to 10 days

C) 14 to 15 days

D) 28 to 30 days

46

Health is a dynamic state of complete physical, mental, and social well-being. It is not only the absence of disease or infirmity. On the other hand, **Public Health** is the science of protecting and improving the health of individuals and their communities.

Which of the following about public health is not correct?

A) Public health refers to what the society does to help the people to be healthy.

B) The primary goal of public health is to help and cure infected people.

C) Public Health Promotion targets the entire population and aims to improve overall health.

D) Assessment, policy development, and assurance are the critical functions of public health.

47

Local departments of public health have very important responsibilities. Which of the following is one of these responsibilities?

A) Training interested community members in emergency first aid.

B) Organizing information about the infectious diseases within the community.

C) Administering physical fitness assessments of public school students.

D) Taking actions to ban unsafe health-related products which are sold in local stores.

48

A **prescription** is an order that tells the pharmacist what medication is needed for the patient.

For which of the following you would most likely need to get a prescription from a doctor?

A) Diet Pills

B) Analgesics

C) Birth control pills

D) Vitamin supplements

49

Human immunodeficiency virus or HIV is a microorganism that targets the immune system of the body, making a person more susceptible to diseases.

Which of the following is a vital risk factor for incurring HIV among sexually active people?

A) Getting an organ transplant or blood transmission

B) Having a concealed hereditary blood disease

C) Being frequently involved in kissing with different people

D) Being sexually engaged to a person with multiple partners

50

Haemophilus influenzae type b (Hib) may cause a life-threatening infection that can lead to severe disease, especially in children.

Which of the following defines Hib best?

A) Fungal infection

B) Viral infection

C) Bacterial infection

D) Immune disease

CONTINUE ▶

51

During physical training, your muscles do their job by pulling on your bones, which function as levers to create movement. First, second and third-class lever are the classifications of levers concerning physical exercises. The third-class lever is the most commonly used exercise in the body, but some use the first and second-class lever.

In the exercises shown below, which of the following involves the first-class lever?

A) Push-ups

B) Biceps curls

C) Triceps pushdown

D) Seated leg extensions

52

Complex carbohydrates consist of a long and complex chain of sugar molecules and they are larger than a simple carbohydrate.

Which of the following is the reason that endurance athletes view complex carbohydrates as an excellent source of energy?

A) An immediate and a timed-release energy source can be provided by complex carbohydrates since they can easily be digested.

B) Complex carbohydrates cannot be depleted from muscles by intense exercise since they are slow to metabolize.

C) The liver can convert complex carbohydrates into triglycerides that are stored throughout the body.

D) Athletes will not easily feel hunger since complex carbohydrates induce a feeling of fullness without adding extra calories.

53

Movement is powered by skeletal muscles, which are attached to the skeleton at various sites on bones. Muscles, bones, and joints provide the principal mechanics for movement, all coordinated by the nervous system.

Which of the following about the skeletal system is not correct?

A) Osteoporosis is a disease that causes bones to become weak and brittle.

B) A tendon is a fibrous connective tissue which attaches muscle to muscle.

C) Arthritis is a disorder of the joints. It involves inflammation of one or more joints.

D) Joints are structures where two bones are attached. A ligament is the fibrous connective tissue that connects bones to other bones.

54

An inflammatory response is usually activated after an injury. Which of the following symptoms is not a sign of inflammation?

A) Pain

B) Redness

C) Bleeding

D) Lose of function

55

Which of the following agencies is responsible for the approval of using azidothymidine (AZT) as the treatment for AIDS?

A) Federal Trade Commission

B) Division of Consumer Affairs

C) Food and Drug Administration

D) Consumer Products Safety Commission

56

The process involving changes in the physical appearance as a child's body undergoes maturity into an adult body is called **puberty**.

In males, which of the following occurs first during puberty?

A) Shoulder widening

B) Changes in the voice

C) The appearance of facial hair

D) Increase in the size of the testes

57

Children need to have good healthy eating patterns to avoid any future health problems.

Which of the following methods would be the most effective in motivating children to practice healthy eating patterns?

A) Foods that are refined or processed are avoided.
B) Foods from all the major groups of food are included in their meals.
C) Candies or anything sweet is offered as a reward upon completing a balanced meal.
D) Fruit beverages are given to them instead of raw or cooked vegetables and fruits.

58

Which of the following is the most likely reason why the effects of air pollution and soil contamination from pesticides usually does not manifest in a short term?

A) Avoiding exposure on such hazards is easy.
B) Its clean up can be done quickly and effectively.
C) Its impact on health tend to develop slowly over time.
D) It affects the animal population first, rather than the human population.

59

Accidental injuries are one of the most frequent causes of death in children.

Which of the following is the most significant risk factor for injuries among children?

A) Lack of education
B) Living in poverty
C) Accident susceptibility
D) Lack of parental supervision

60

Patients exhibiting symptoms of flu have been increasing and are being treated by the health-care practitioners in the community. However, the patients do not respond to any of the standard medications for the treatment of flu.

In this case, which of the following agencies should these practitioners contact for assistance?

A) American Medical Association
B) American Pharmacists Association
C) Centers for Disease Control and Prevention
D) Center for Drug Evaluation and Research

CONTINUE ▶

61

Which of the following best describes the shared function of the nervous system and the endocrine system?

A) To activate the reproductive glands
B) To regulate the development and growth.
C) To regulate the communication within the body
D) To control the balance of blood pressure and water in the body

62

Which of the following best states why alcohol use increases the chance of injury for people involved in recreational activities?

A) Alcohol use heightens sensory perception and causes substantial exaggerated responses.
B) Alcoholic beverages contain elements that hasten metabolism.
C) Alcoholic drinks contain ethanol or ethyl alcohol, a type of psychoactive drug.
D) Alcohol usage weakens motor reflexes and slows down time reception.

63

Waste treatment refers to the activities required to ensure that waste has the least possible impact on the environment.

Which of the following best describes the primary objective of Reduce, Reuse, and Recycle in waste treatment hierarchy?

A) Combining the spillover costs of a particular product into its market price.

B) Guaranteeing that costs of waste disposal are paid fairly by the waste generators.

C) Gaining a maximum benefit from products and at the same time, making a minimal amount of waste.

D) Giving incentives in regards to the correct allocation of non-hazardous wastes, both commercial and industrial.

64

When lead builds up in the body, **lead poisoning** occurs and it can cause serious health problems.

Which of the following in older dwellings can be one of the reasons of lead poisoning?

A) Insulation materials on the walls

B) Paint on the walls and woodwork

C) Frayed electrical wirings and switches

D) Corroded pipes and channels of heating and cooling systems

65

Decomposing organic matter recycles various organic materials otherwise regarded as waste products.

Which of the following processes decomposes plant remains into humus by naturally occurring soil bacteria?

A) Mulching

B) Reducing

C) Conserving

D) Composting

66

Vitamins are the organic compounds that we need in small quantities to sustain our life.

Which of the following about vitamins is true?

A) Biotin is known as vitamin H.

B) Folate is a water soluble vitamin B.

C) Vitamin is an essential micronutrient.

D) All of the above

67

A **personality disorder** refers to a long-term pattern of thinking and behavior that causes distress, making it difficult to function in everyday life.

In other words, which of the following best describes the condition?

A) Personality disorders are the person's reactions to stress.

B) Personality disorders are maladaptive ways of perceiving, thinking, and relating.

C) Personality disorders are episodic in nature.

D) Personality disorders are intra-psychic disturbances.

68

In human beings, the homeostatic regulation of body temperature involves such mechanisms as sweating when the internal temperature becomes excessive and shivering to produce heat, as well as the generation of heat through metabolic processes when the internal temperature falls too low.

Which of the following is not included in homeostatic mechanisms in the body?

A) Excretion

B) Respiration

C) Osmoregulation

D) Thermoregulation

69

Catabolism is the breakdown of complex molecules in living organisms to form simpler ones.

Which of the following about catabolism is true?

A) Digestion is a catabolic reaction.

B) Catabolism is a destructive metabolism.

C) Catabolic reactions involve the release of energy.

D) All of the above.

70

The 33 individual, interlocking bones that form the spinal column is called the **vertebrae**.

Which of the following is not correct about vertebrae?

A) There are twelve thoracic vertebrae from the middle to upper back.

B) Five lunar vertebrae make up the lower back.

C) There are seven cervical vertebrae in the neck region.

D) There are five sacral vertebrae, which are fused together.

Which of the following is representing an incorrect statement?

A) Water comprises 70% or more of the bodies of animals.

B) Fats yield the most significant amount of energy.

C) Proteins are the facilitators of growth and repair of animal cells and are also a form of reserved energy.

D) Carbohydrates are the least essential type of nutrient the body needs.

Sulfur dioxide and nitrogen oxide emission causes acid rain by reacting with the water molecules in the atmosphere to produce acids.

Which of the following about the acid rains is not correct?

A) Ammonia is produced by the reaction of sulfurous gases such as sulfur dioxide with water.

B) Deceased fish and wildlife populations, damaged bodies of water, as well as human health hazards has been linked by scientific evidence to acid rain.

C) Acid rain is a 1980s household term used when emissions from the industry and motor vehicles were being blamed for causing environmental deterioration.

D) Acid rain results from air pollution since sulfur dioxide and nitrogen oxides are bi-products of burning fuels in electric utilities as well as other industrial and natural sources.

Alcoholism is the term used for any drinking of alcohol that results in mental or physical health problems.

Which of the following describes alcoholism?

A) Alcohol intolerance

B) Hard-drinking on weekends

C) The inability to control the amount a person drinks.

D) None of the above

Minerals needed by the body can be classified as macrominerals (those needed in large amounts) and trace minerals (those needed in small amounts).

Which of the following statements is correct about minerals?

A) Both zinc and sodium are trace minerals.

B) Both zinc and sodium are macrominerals

C) Zinc is a trace mineral while sodium is a macromineral.

D) Zinc is a macromineral while sodium is a trace mineral.

The term used to describe the amount of blood the heart pumps through the circulatory system within a minute is **cardiac output**. On the other hand, stroke volume is the amount of blood put out by the left ventricle of the heart in one contraction. In general, the stroke volume and the heart rate regulate the cardiac output.

How can cardiac output (Q) be measured?

A) The quantity of oxygen consumed times the heart's rate of pumping.

B) The quantity of oxygen consumed times the pressure exerted against the arterial walls.

C) The quantity of blood ejected with each beat times the pressure exerted against the artery walls.

D) The quantity of blood ejected with each beat times the heart's rate of pumping.

A person's number of breaths per minute is called **respiratory rate**. If a person has 25 breaths per minute, it is considered as abnormal.

Which of the following respiratory rate is considered to be normal?

A) 6 to 10 breaths per minute

B) 16 to 20 breaths per minute

C) 22 to 26 breaths per minute

D) 30 to 36 breaths per minute

CONTINUE ▶

77

Alcoholic beverages are drinks that contain a considerable amount of ethanol which is considered as a depressant.

As alcohol enters the body, in which of the following body organs is it metabolized?

A) In the liver
B) In the brain
C) In the kidneys
D) In the stomach

78

Carbohydrates serve as the immediate energy source of our body. Corns, wheat, oats, and barley fall in which of the following classification of carbohydrates?

A) Starch
B) Glycogen
C) Glycoprotein
D) Oligosaccharide

79

Skin is the soft outer tissue covering of vertebrates. It has three main functions; protection, regulation, and sensation.

Which of the following about skin is not defined correctly?

A) Collagen is is the most abundant protein in our bodies which gives our skin strength and elasticity.
B) The epidermis is the thin, top layer of the skin that contains blood vessels, lymph vessels, hair follicles, and glands.
C) Sebum is an oily substance that is secreted by the sebaceous glands that help keep the skin and hair moisturized.
D) Keratin is found in hair, horns, claws, hooves, and the outer layer of human skin which serves as a waterproofing protein in the skin.

Human activities are partly responsible for changes in global temperatures experienced during the past 100 years.

Which of the following best explains why average global temperatures over the last 100 years is so high?

A) Natural systems do not generally shift that quickly unless disturbed by some external mechanism.

B) Natural systems are always changing, but generally at an almost constant rate.

C) Natural systems usually show randomly fluctuating rates of change over time.

D) Natural systems usually show decreasing rates of change as the system matures.

CONTINUE ▶

SECTION 6 - GENERAL HEALTH

#	Answer	Topic	Subtopic	#	Answer	Topic	Subtopic	#	Answer	Topic	Subtopic	#	Answer	Topic	Subtopic
1	B	TC	S3	21	B	TC	S4	41	C	TC	S2	61	C	TC	S6
2	B	TC	S3	22	C	TC	S4	42	C	TC	S7	62	D	TC	S2
3	D	TC	S7	23	C	TC	S1	43	B	TC	S2	63	C	TC	S5
4	B	TC	S7	24	D	TC	S6	44	B	TC	S7	64	B	TC	S5
5	D	TC	S3	25	C	TC	S5	45	D	TC	S6	65	D	TC	S5
6	B	TC	S2	26	C	TC	S7	46	B	TC	S3	66	D	TC	S4
7	B	TC	S3	27	D	TC	S7	47	B	TC	S3	67	B	TC	S2
8	A	TC	S4	28	A	TC	S4	48	C	TC	S1	68	B	TC	S6
9	A	TC	S7	29	B	TC	S1	49	D	TC	S7	69	D	TC	S4
10	C	TC	S1	30	C	TC	S7	50	C	TC	S7	70	B	TC	S6
11	B	TC	S4	31	B	TC	S2	51	C	TC	S6	71	D	TC	S4
12	A	TC	S3	32	D	TC	S6	52	A	TC	S4	72	A	TC	S5
13	A	TC	S2	33	B	TC	S2	53	B	TC	S6	73	C	TC	S1
14	C	TC	S2	34	C	TC	S7	54	C	TC	S7	74	C	TC	S4
15	B	TC	S7	35	C	TC	S2	55	C	TC	S7	75	D	TC	S6
16	B	TC	S4	36	B	TC	S6	56	D	TC	S6	76	B	TC	S6
17	C	TC	S3	37	B	TC	S4	57	B	TC	S4	77	A	TC	S6
18	B	TC	S4	38	B	TC	S5	58	C	TC	S5	78	A	TC	S4
19	B	TC	S4	39	B	TC	S7	59	B	TC	S7	79	B	TC	S6
20	B	TC	S2	40	A	TC	S3	60	C	TC	S3	80	A	TC	S5

Topics & Subtopics

Code	Description	Code	Description
SC1	Personal Health	SC5	Environmental Health
SC2	Mental & Emotional Health	SC6	Anatomy & Physiology
SC3	Community Health	SC7	Health Promotion & Prevention of Injury and Diseases
SC4	Nutrition Health	TC	General Health

CONTINUE ▶

TEST DIRECTION

Read the questions carefully and then choose the ONE best answer to each question.

Be sure to allocate your time carefully so you are able to complete the entire test within the testing session. You may go back and review your answers at any time.

You may use any available space in your test booklet for scratch work.

Questions in this booklet are not actual test questions but they are the samples for commonly asked questions.

This test aims to cover all topics which may appear on the actual test. However some topics may not be covered.

Studying this booklet will be preparing you for the actual test. It will not guarantee improving your test score but it will help you pass your exam on the first attempt.

Some useful tips for answering multiple choice questions;

- Start with the questions that you can easily answer.

- Underline the keywords in the question.

- Be sure to read all the choices given.

- Watch for keywords such as NOT, always, only, all, never, completely.

- Do not forget to answer every question.

1

Which of the following about the sports is not correct?

A) Bocce, sometimes anglicized as bocci, is a target game.

B) Aerobics, Basketball, Cricket are all Olympic Sports.

C) Badminton is a net/wall game in the same class as tennis, volleyball, racquetball, and handball.

D) Lacrosse and Basketball, which involve shooting the ball at a target or goal, are considered invasion games because of their nature of the offensive and defensive play.

2

The Olympic motto Citius, Altius, Fortius in Latin stands for which of the following?

A) Big, Bigger, Biggest

B) Look, Observe, Win

C) Faster, Higher, Stronger

D) Lighter, Stronger, Winner

3

Attribution theory of motivation explains why people do what they do. Bernard Weiner states that people seek causal factors that allow them to maintain a positive self-image, and it is these attributions that determine an individual's motivation to repeat behaviors.

According to the attribution motivational theory, which of the following do physical education teachers expect from their students?

A) To be motivated intrinsically

B) To be motivated extrinsically

C) To ascribe their successes and failures to factors within their own control

D) To ascribe their successes and failures to factors outside their own control

4

According to World Health Organization, **musculoskeletal problems** mainly contribute to disability worldwide, with low back pain being the single major cause of disability globally.

Which of the following abilities can be identified from data assessment of an individual's potential of developing musculoskeletal problems and performing daily activities?

A) Stamina

B) Flexibility

C) Coordination

D) Muscle strength

5

The ball is a solid or hollow sphere or ovoid, especially one that is kicked, thrown, or hit in a game.

Which of the following types of the ball should a teacher use to improve catching skills of preschool students who are struggling to catch an 8.5-inch playground ball?

A) Foam ball
B) Basketball
C) Tennis ball
D) Golf ball

6

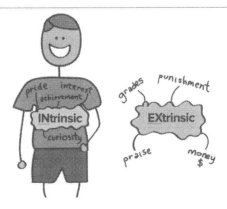

Motivation helps students achieve high levels of performance and overcome barriers in order to change.

Which of the following helps enhancing student motivation in physical education settings?

A) Comparing performance among peers.
B) Providing opportunities for self determination through choice.
C) Assigning easily accomplished tasks that guarantee success.
D) Following familiar and predictable structures in the activities.

7

If a person engages in a vigorous physical activity in which of the following will there be an increase?

A) Resting heart rate
B) Coronary thrombosis
C) Low density lipoproteins
D) High density lipoproteins

8

When training for basketball games, the player has to acquire the basic maneuvers such as passing and screening to ensure that he can be of help during the play. The coach or an appointed teammate can call the play.

Which of the following is a maneuver when an offensive player passes to a teammate and then immediately cuts in toward the basket for a return pass?

A) Pick
B) Switching
C) Give-and-go
D) Catch-and-shoot

9

A non-locomotor skill can simply be used to move the different body parts without the need to move from the current position continuously.

Which of the following non-locomotor skills refers to the sharp change of direction from one's original line of movement?

A) Dodging
B) Swaying
C) Swinging
D) Twisting

10

Which of the following represents angular motion?

A) The knees of a cyclist
B) The legs of a runner
C) The arms of a swimmer
D) All of the above

CONTINUE ▶

11

Which of the following factors affects the speed of an object thrown overhand?

A) Grip-release
B) Wrist Flexion
C) Hip rotation
D) Hand-held proximity

12

Each school publishes it own periodicals about physical activities to help students catch-up on what is happening around them and encourage them to become more interested in all of the physical activities that they offer.

Which of the following periodicals publish research in physical education?

A) PTA Notes
B) School PE Update
C) Community Weekly Reports
D) Journal of Physical Education

13

The **progression** starts on a slow and cautious exercise program before proceeding to more rigorous activities.

Which of the following situations applies the concept of progression?

A) Start with a stretching program every day.
B) Start with a stretching program with ten sets of reps.
C) Start with a stretching program with high respiratory rate activity.
D) Start with a stretching program holding stretches for 30 seconds and work up to holding stretches for 90 seconds.

14

Muscle is defined as a bundle of fibrous tissue in a body with the ability to contract or produce movements.

Which of the following refers to the ability for a muscle to repeatedly contract over a period of time?

A) Muscle growth
B) Muscle stability
C) Muscle strength
D) Muscle endurance

15

Non-locomotor skills are the bodily movements that can be produced without actually moving from your current position. A simple shake of the hands can be considered as a non-locomotor skill.

Which of the following non-locomotor skill entails movement around a joint where two body parts meet?

A) Bending
B) Swaying
C) Twisting
D) Stretching

16

Overloaded exercise is recommended to those students who wish to improve faster. The exercise principle offers such benefits, but the risk is also heavy, depending on the student's bodily capacity.

Which of the following indicators does not modify 'overload?'

A) Intensity
B) Frequency
C) Effort exerted
D) Length of time

17

Aerobic exercise is any bodily movement that aims to develop cardiovascular conditioning. It is associated with an increased intake of oxygen and faster heart rate.

Which of the following is not developed or improved in an aerobic dance?

A) Flexibility
B) Body composition
C) Body coordination
D) Cardio-respiratory function

18

Sports is primarily considered as what type of activity as described by most sports sociologists?

A) Generalized
B) Professionalized
C) Idealized
D) Institutionalized

19

The human body's physiology includes the aspects of nutrient intake, energy output, and overall body movement in everyday life. The shape of the body can be determined by the movement, food intake, and energy output.

Which of the following is a physiological benefit of exercise?

A) Cardiac hypertrophy

B) Quicker recovery rate

C) Reducing mental tension

D) Improving muscle strength

20

The fitness training principle of progressive overload is best illustrated in which of the following personal fitness plan situations?

A) Doing a more varied exercise routine

B) Slowly raising the strength or duration of exercise sessions

C) Trying different time spans between exercise sessions

D) Always allowing little or no rest between exercise sessions

21

Ball games are one of the major sports that people are inclined to.

Which of the following skills will students develop when hitting a large balloon with both hands?

A) Striking

B) Flapping

C) Dribbling

D) Volleying

22

Some non-locomotor skills differ in their orientation. Most of them can be done by standing up, while some are also done by bending or sitting.

Which of the following non-locomotor skills is developed by letting a student naturally fall down on his own while letting him be aware of how he falls?

A) Falling

B) Shaking

C) Dodging

D) Swinging

23

Swimming is a physical activity that involves the whole body. It is performed on water and aims to cover a distance in the water by using appropriate bodily movements.

Which of the following can determine the skill level achievement of a student in swimming?

A) How long can a student float

B) How deep a student can dive

C) How many strokes it took to swim a distance

D) How fast can a student swim a distance using freestyle

24

Which of the following skills is the reason why the activity patterns of a five-year-old child are more physically demanding than younger children?

A) Social skills

B) Cognitive skills

C) Gross-motor skills

D) Manipulative skills

25

Tennis is a similar sport to badminton but it uses a rubber-type ball that bounces on the lawn court. The players have to return the ball to the side of the court until one of them drops or fails to return it.

Which of the following shot should a defensive player who is still returning to the court apply to gain more time for the act?

A) Lob shot

B) Dink shot

C) Drop shot

D) Down-the-line shot

26

Process assessment is a subjective and observational approach to correct a student's error in skills presentation. It is not necessarily the best correction, but it can be more appropriate, depending on the instructor.

Which of the following errors is not identified by process assessment?

A) Style

B) Form

C) End result

D) Mechanics

CONTINUE ▶

27

When physical education was being introduced in the US, most students viewed it as another form of playing rather than a class discussion. It also includes training for sports events.

Which of the following states first introduced physical education?

A) Iowa

B) Kansas

C) California

D) Florida

28

Which of the following assessment accomplishes a subjective, observational approach to identify errors in the form, style, or mechanics of a skill?

A) Process assessment

B) Product assessment

C) Criterion-referenced tests

D) Standardized norm-referenced tests

Equilibrium refers to a balanced state with no net tendency towards change. In mechanics;

• when no force acts to make a body move in a line, the body is in **translational equilibrium.**

• when no force acts to make the body turn, the body is in **rotational equilibrium.**

• when a body is in equilibrium while at rest, it is in **static equilibrium.**

Which of the following conditions does not enhance equilibrium to balance forces?

A) Increasing the base of support.
B) Lowering the center of support and increasing the base of support.
C) Shifting the center of gravity away from the direction of movement.
D) None of the above

A **goalkeep**er is responsible for preventing the opposing team from scoring by blocking or intercepting goal shots. In turn, he must need a good response to change.

Which of the following refers to the ability of the body to rapidly change the direction?

A) Agility
B) Stamina
C) Flexibility
D) Reaction time

CONTINUE ▶

31

A student's performance is measured in a few metrics, such as speed, time, distance, and reach. Other factors may include reaction time, vertical jump, and arms reach.

Which of the following is not a skills assessment test?

A) Iowa Brace Test
B) Rodgers Strength Test
C) AAHPERD Youth Fitness Test
D) US Open Qualitative Jumping Examination

32

Which of the following does a soccer player exhibit when he decided to kick the ball in an open space or the area wherein none of his opponents is present?

A) Management
B) Mastery
C) Strategy
D) Exhibition

33

Physical Education (PE) is the systematic instruction in sports, exercises, and hygiene given as part of a school or college program. The six strands in the PE curriculum are;

- Motor and Sports Skills,
- Health and Fitness,
- Sport-related Values and Attitudes,
- Knowledge and Practice of Safety,
- Knowledge of Movement,
- Aesthetic Sensitivity.

Which of the following about PE is not correct?

A) It is an important part of whole person development and "educates students through physical activities".

B) It helps students pursue an active and healthy lifestyle, develops generic skills, and nurtures positive values and attitudes.

C) It helps students develop related skills, knowledge, and attitudes for leading and enjoying an active and healthy lifestyle.

D) Physical Education is "education through the physical" and "Physically passive" is the central aim of it.

34

The concepts used in Physical Education can be as complex as a mathematical formula if not used appropriately. The instructor must be able to provide subsequent goals to develop and explain concepts of skills.

Which of the following concept involves students making decisions about an object's positional changes in space?

A) Body Awareness
B) Spatial Awareness
C) Cognitive Awareness
D) Motion-Vision Awareness

215

CONTINUE ▶

35

Sports athletes and enthusiasts are protected by law. Corruption and other forms of illegal contact from outsiders are prohibited under this law.

Which of the professional organization protects amateur sports from corruption?

A) Amateur Athletic Union
B) National Collegiate Athletic Association
C) Association for Intercollegiate Athletics for Women
D) American Alliance for Health, Physical Education, Recreation and Dance

36

In physical education (PE) there are many modes of assessments which inform future planning and teaching. Assessment is essential and integral to effective teaching and learning in PE as it provides information on students' strengths, weaknesses, and educational requirements,

Which of the following about assessment in PE is correct?

A) It is expected that all PE teachers implement a range of assessment methods in every lesson.
B) For an effective assessment, it is important for the criteria to be precise, clearly identified, and related to each other.
C) Strong observational skills, detailed knowledge of activities and their techniques are important for a PE teacher to develop a reliable assessment.
D) All of the above

What factor is developed when a person is swimming ½ mile four times a week?

A) Agility

B) Balance

C) Flexibility

D) Aerobic Fitness

Bowling is a ball-type sport which requires the student to throw and let the ball roll on a bowling alley towards the pins at the end. The student is required to practice footwork and effective throwing and rolling skills.

Which of the following can be used to assess skill achievement level in bowling?

A) Calculating a student's average

B) Calculating how many spares were thrown

C) Calculating how many bowling balls were thrown

D) Calculating how fast and far the bowling bowls were thrown

Skill refers to the ability to use a person's knowledge to perform in coordination.

Which of the following skills is incorrectly associated?

A) Dancing refers to move one's body rhythmically through a series of steps.

B) Trapping refers to propelling an object through the air with a rapid movement of the arm and wrist.

C) Jumping refers to the movement of letting one's body off of the ground for a short time using his or her power.

D) None of the above

Manipulative skills are used to manipulate objects. Redirecting an object from its original direction is a type of manipulative skill.

Which of the following manipulative skills use the hands to stop the momentum of an object?

A) Rolling

B) Striking

C) Catching

D) Trapping

41

In 1866, the first public school to require physical education for its curriculum was introduced in the US. The revised curriculum was devised to improve the physical condition of the youth in the country.

Which of the following year did the first private school (Round Hill School) require physical education in its curriculum?

A) 1799
B) 1808
C) 1823
D) 1827

42

A **meet** is a small event of different sports competitions that may include one or more schools. The number of sports and participants is limited as much as possible.

Which of the following is not a type of meet?

A) Lateral
B) Intramural
C) Extramural
D) Interscholastic

43

The beat is defined as a rhythmic movement or is the speed at which a piece of music is played.

Which of the following is musical note played by a student when he claps in each beat twice in an even rhythm of eight-beat measure?

A) Eighth notes
B) Sixteenth notes
C) Quarter notes
D) Downbeats

44

Long-term planning refers to the setting of goals for the period of physical education. Steps must be taken to achieve the set goal by planning the activities of the students.

Which of the following management techniques is not essential to long-term planning?

A) Parental observation
B) Progress evaluation
C) Physical performance
D) Precise activity planning

45

Task cards are a set of cards that have tasks or questions written on them.

When teaching physical education skills, which of the following is the main advantage of using commercially-prepared task cards?

A) Students can refer to the cards as needed for written cues and visual images of proper techniques.

B) Information on cards can easily be changed in case of corrections to the lessons.

C) Evaluation of the students' performance can be tracked and managed faster.

D) Teachers can be assured that students will demonstrate consistency in performing skills.

46

What should teachers keep in mind when designing instruction?

A) Not all kids are at the same level.

B) All students understand the same way.

C) Instructional planning isn't as crucial as it is believed.

D) The previous experiences of students aren't the base of learning.

47

A student reports that another student in the class is carrying a pocketknife. Which of the following actions would be most appropriate for the teacher to take?

A) Contact the school administrator immediately to remove the student from the classroom.

B) Request that the accused student come into the hall and empty all pockets.

C) Advise the student's parents of the report and ask how they wish the situation to be handled.

D) Investigate the incident further by seeking corroboration of the report from other students.

48

Communication is exchanging information by speaking, writing, or using some other medium.

Which of the following is not correct about communication?

A) Nonverbal communication is the use of body movements to send a message.

B) If a speaker uses graphs, charts he is using an assertion of logic.

C) It is never appropriate to use obscene language in a speech.

D) Pitch has a psychological effect that influences how people perceive your speech's content.

49

Plyometric exercises are considered as an effective way to improve strength and speed which is beneficial for sports training.

Which of the following is the most appropriate surface when performing high-intensity, low body plyometric drills?

A) Artificial turf

B) Grass field

C) Mini trampoline

D) Indoor basketball court

50

Knowing workout and exercise goal is a critical step in creating the best workout routine.

To help a student establish individual fitness goals, which of the following should be a teacher's initial step?

A) Evaluate student's pre-fitness test.

B) Watch the student performs fitness test.

C) Assess the health-related fitness levels of the student.

D) Survey the student's family about his/her physical activity levels.

51

Formative assessment refers to a wide variety of methods that teachers use to conduct in-process evaluations.

Which of the following is the main advantage formative assessment strategies?

A) Provide teachers the comparison for student's individual and group learning.

B) Provide a copy of the basis of evaluation of parents to the learning of their children.

C) Provide both teachers and students with invaluable information about what students understand, and what they don't.

D) Provide standardized data that captures the degree to which students have achieved learning outcomes.

CONTINUE ▶

52

During the start of the school year, which of the following lists are the best practices to be followed by a PE teacher to establish good classroom management?

A) Posting rules on the wall, not smiling and learning the names of the students.

B) Teaching students a predetermined signal to stop activity, establishing rules and reviewing them with the students, creating a record-keeping system

C) Posting rules on the wall, creating a record-keeping system and having an open gym period

D) Learning the names of the students, playing fun games with the students and teaching the class how to do warm-ups

53

In developing a manual of safety procedures for a physical education program, which of the following should be included?

I. Teachers must mark appropriate traffic patterns around the throwing area in javelin classes.

II. Students must read and sign a copy of the rules for archery classes.

III. Before soccer classes start, teachers must personally inspect playing fields.

IV. During aerobic fitness activities, students must exercise at or below 50% of their maximal heart rate.

A) I and III

B) II and IV

C) I, II and III

D) II, III, and IV

54

The forehand in tennis is a shot made by swinging the racket across one's body with the hand moving palm-first. On the other hand, **backhand** is a stroke played with the back of the hand facing in the direction of the stroke, typically starting with the arm crossing the body.

In order to allow a player to contact the ball in front of the body, there must be a pivot on the back foot and a step towards the net.

Which of the following is the most suitable technique before contacting the ball?

A) Keeping back straight while bending knees

B) Making sure that the rotation of racquet is counterclockwise

C) Pointing the top of the racquet towards the opponent

D) Turning the shoulders early in preparation for the swing

55

health. moves. minds.

Why is Society of Health and Physical Educators (SHAPE America) considered an important resource for beginning physical educators?

A) Because it disseminates current information in order to enhance the knowledge about physical education and improve practice

B) Because it allows access to a blog that allows parents, students, and teachers to cooperate with each other

C) Because it provides liability insurance for physical education once a problem comes up

D) Because its website contains all the necessary lesson plans that can be used by a physical education teacher

56

Bernard Weiner, who is an American social psychologist, created **the attribution theory of motivation** as a framework to explain why people do what they do. He states that people seek causal factors that allow them to maintain a positive self-image, and it is these attributions that determine an individual's motivation to repeat behaviors.

According to the attribution motivational theory, which of the following actions of a physical education teacher is true?

A) Motivating students by external rewards.

B) Motivating students by interest or enjoyment without relying on external rewards.

C) Attributing students' successes and failures to factors within their own control.

D) Attributing students' successes and failures to factors outside their own control.

57

In order to set appropriate health-related goals, which of the following assessment techniques will most likely help students?

A) Completing a fitness test

B) Computing every calorie intake

C) Keeping track of other students' improvement on their training

D) Reading journals, books, and essays about sports and sport rules

58

Physical Strength is generated through the interaction of muscles, skeleton, tendons, and ligaments and through energy conversion in the muscles. After the age of 20, both males and females achieve their maximum physical strength.

Which of the following could be accounted for this change at that age level?

A) A free radical formation is fastest

B) The rate of metabolism is slowest

C) Muscular cross-sectional areas are largest

D) Degradation of muscles has started to take place

59

The belayer is the person on the ground who secures the climber, keeping a close eye on the climber's progress and letting out slack to the line by releasing the belay.

In indoor rock climbing, which of the following should a belayer do to make sure the climber is safe?

A) Reminding the climber to hold closer to the edge

B) Instructing the climber where and when to take a step

C) Keeping the brake hand in the "lock off" position when there is no slack or movement by the climber

D) Maintaining a secure position beneath the climber and as close to the wall as possible.

60

An open motor skill is a skill which is performed in an unstable environment where the start point is determined by the environment.

Which of the following describes an open motor skill?

A) The participant often performs the skill in an unpredictable, changing environment

B) The participant often performs the skill in an environment with constant conditions

C) The skill can be performed in precisely the same way each time regardless of the context

D) Open motor skills are typically easier to perform as they involve less variability and complexity of factors to be accounted for

Physical fitness is a state of health and well-being and, more specifically, the ability to perform aspects of sports, occupations and daily activities. Physical fitness is generally achieved through proper nutrition, moderate-vigorous physical exercise, and sufficient rest.

Which of the following would be the most appropriate action to develop a cognitive lesson that includes health-enhancing physical fitness to 8th-grade students?

A) Instruct students to survey each other's level of physical fitness

B) Instruct students to create a webpage demonstrating an understanding of the fitness components.

C) Instruct students to assess their fitness levels with a help of a parent or guardian

D) Instruct students to have a one-mile fitness assessment with a heart rate monitor

Sidearm is a motion for throwing a ball along a low, approximately horizontal axis rather than a high, mostly vertical axis (overhand).

Which of the following would be the most appropriate advice of a baseball coach while he is teaching his students on the most important element in doing a two-handed side-arm strike to bat a ball?

A) "Keep your bat near the ground and create 90-degree angle when the ball is thrown."

B) "Keep your batting elbow flexed during the entire swing and stop the follow-through at the point of contact."

C) "Hold the bat above your shoulder and quickly transfer your body weight sidewards."

D) "Transfer your weight from your back foot to your front foot as your hips and shoulder rotate into the swing."

## 63

The underhand throw is performed with the hand below the level of the elbow or the arm below the level of the shoulder.

Which of the following is the most suitable technique when a teacher is teaching a children to throw a ball using an underhand throw?

A) Bring dominant hand back until the height of elbow is equal to the height of shoulder while facing dominant arm upward at a 90-degree angle.

B) Holding the ball with both hands at your chest with both fingers spread around the ball

C) Taking one step forward with the foot opposite the throwing hand

D) Positioning both feet on the ground, taking the ball in both hands back and over the head, and without breaking your momentum, releasing the ball with both hands

## 64

Cardiopulmonary resuscitation or CPR is an emergency technique used on someone whose heart or breathing has stopped. This is commonly used in emergency situations like a heart attack or near drowning.

In the following sequence of procedure in doing the protocol of CPR, which choice has the correct sequence?

1. Open airway

2. Check to breathe

3. Supply two full breaths

4. Check pulse

A) 1 - 4 - 3 - 2
B) 2 - 4 - 1 - 3
C) 2 - 3 - 4 - 1
D) 1 - 2 - 3 - 4

SECTION 7 - PHYSICAL EDUCATION

#	Answer	Topic	Subtopic	#	Answer	Topic	Subtopic	#	Answer	Topic	Subtopic	#	Answer	Topic	Subtopic
1	B	TB	S3	17	A	TB	S4	33	D	TB	S2	49	B	TB	S4
2	C	TB	S6	18	D	TB	S3	34	B	TB	S3	50	C	TB	S1
3	C	TB	S7	19	C	TB	S2	35	A	TB	S3	51	C	TB	S1
4	B	TB	S5	20	B	TB	S4	36	D	TB	S5	52	B	TB	S1
5	A	TB	S3	21	D	TB	S4	37	D	TB	S2	53	C	TB	S3
6	B	TB	S7	22	A	TB	S4	38	A	TB	S5	54	D	TB	S3
7	D	TB	S4	23	C	TB	S5	39	B	TB	S3	55	A	TB	S1
8	C	TB	S1	24	C	TB	S2	40	C	TB	S3	56	C	TB	S1
9	A	TB	S2	25	A	TB	S2	41	C	TB	S7	57	A	TB	S2
10	D	TB	S3	26	C	TB	S5	42	A	TB	S3	58	C	TB	S3
11	C	TB	S3	27	C	TB	S6	43	B	TB	S3	59	C	TB	S3
12	D	TB	S1	28	A	TB	S5	44	A	TB	S3	60	A	TB	S2
13	D	TB	S3	29	C	TB	S4	45	A	TB	S1	61	B	TB	S2
14	D	TB	S4	30	A	TB	S3	46	A	TB	S1	62	D	TB	S3
15	A	TB	S2	31	D	TB	S5	47	A	TB	S6	63	C	TB	S3
16	C	TB	S2	32	C	TB	S3	48	D	TB	S6	64	D	TB	S3

Topics & Subtopics

Code	Description	Code	Description
SB1	Planning Instruction	SB5	Student Assessment
SB2	Student Growth & Development	SB6	Communication, Collaboration & Technology
SB3	Planning Activities	SB7	Management & Motivation
SB4	Health-Related Physical Fitness	TB	Physical Education

CONTINUE ▶

75487818R00138